Undoing the Enemy's Snares

Breaking Cycles That Hold You Back and Discovering Lasting Freedom

By Jared Gregory

Defining Media Group LLC

Copyright © 2025 by Jared Gregory | The Defining Media Group LLC
All rights reserved.

No part of this publication may be reproduced, stored in a retrieval system, or transmitted in any form or by any means—electronic, mechanical, photocopying, recording, or otherwise—without the prior written permission of the publisher, except in the case of brief quotations used in reviews, teaching, or discussion, as permitted by U.S. copyright law.

Published by The Defining Media Group LLC
www.thedefiningplace.com

First Edition
Print Edition: 979-8-9992081-2-5
Ebook ISBN: 979-8-9992081-3-2
Spanish edition in development

This book is intended for educational and informational purposes only. It is not a substitute for professional advice, diagnosis, or treatment. The authors and contributors are not licensed medical, psychological, or legal professionals, and this book is not intended to provide medical, mental health, or legal services.

While every effort has been made to ensure the accuracy and biblical soundness of the content, the authors and publisher make no guarantees and assume no liability for any errors or omissions. The reader is encouraged to seek appropriate professional help when dealing with medical conditions, mental health concerns, or other complex personal issues.

Any stories, testimonies, or experiences shared in this book are for illustrative purposes only and may not reflect typical outcomes. Individual experiences will vary. By reading this book, you agree that neither the authors, The Defining Media Group LLC, associated ministries, nor any contributors shall be held liable for any damages or adverse outcomes resulting from the application of information presented herein.

For crisis support in the U.S., call or text 988, or chat at 988lifeline.org (24/7, confidential). TTY: 711, then 988; ASL Videophone available; Spanish services offered.

Unless otherwise noted, all Scripture quotations are taken from the Holy Bible, New International Version®, NIV®. Copyright © 1973, 1978, 1984, 2011 by Biblica, Inc.™ Used by permission. All rights reserved worldwide.

A Pastoral Acknowledgment & Safety Note

We're honored you're opening your heart to God. Some readers carry stories of grief, trauma, anxiety, intrusive thoughts, or addiction. You are not alone, and seeking help is a sign of courage, not failure. The tools in this book are meant to complement—not replace—professional care from licensed medical and mental-health providers. They are also intended to work alongside pastoral care, discipleship, and deliverance ministry.

When to seek additional help (sooner rather than later):

- Persistent depression, anxiety, panic, trauma flashbacks, or insomnia
- Thoughts of self-harm or suicide, harming others, or feeling unable to stay safe
- Substance misuse, eating disorders, or significant changes in thinking/behavior
- Any medical or psychological symptom that concerns you or those who love you

If you are in immediate danger in the U.S., call 911.

If you're thinking about suicide or are in emotional distress, **call or text 988**, or **chat at 988lifeline.org** for free, confidential support 24/7. TTY users can dial **711**, **then 988**; ASL users can access an ASL Videophone option. Spanish services are available.

Outside the U.S., please contact your local emergency number and crisis services.

We embrace wise, integrated care.

We bless pastoral ministry, discipleship, and deliverance **alongside** physicians, therapists, and counselors. **Do not stop or change medications** without speaking with your prescribing clinician.

Scope & responsibility.

This resource is for educational and ministry purposes and does not constitute medical, mental health, or legal advice. Use these tools with pastoral covering and, when needed, with licensed professionals. Your choices remain your responsibility; use discretion and seek appropriate help.

Table of Contents

A Pastoral Acknowledgment & Safety Note...3
Table of Contents..5
Preface..7
    The Problem This Book Seeks to Address..7
    Other Tensions For Why This Book Is Necessary..8
    Who I Am and How I Came To This Work...8
    Let Me Be Clear About Therapy and Medicine's Role..9
    Who This Resource Is For..9
Introduction..11
    Before You Begin...11
    Tools to Help You Exit The Destructive Patterns You're Stuck In.........................11
Understanding Snares:
How Destructive Patterns and Strongholds Form...13
    The 5 Minute RESET Quickstart..14
    A Full Session Consists of 6 Steps..15
    Key Scriptures For Freedom..21
    A Final Reminder Before Beginning..21
Part 2: Detailed Examination of the 26 Destructive Loops...23
    OVERVIEW OF THE ENEMY'S 26 DESTRUCTIVE LOOPS................................25
    ABANDONMENT LOOP RESET..29
    ACCUSATION LOOP RESET..30
    ANGER LOOP RESET..32
    APATHY LOOP RESET...33
    BETRAYAL LOOP RESET...34
    BITTERNESS LOOP RESET...35
    COMPARISON LOOP RESET...36
    CONTROL LOOP RESET..37
    FEAR LOOP RESET...38
    GRIEF LOOP RESET..39
    IDENTITY CONFUSION LOOP RESET...40
    IDOLATRY LOOP RESET...41
    ISOLATION LOOP RESET..42
    NUMBNESS LOOP RESET...43
    OVERWHELM LOOP RESET..44
    PERFECTIONISM OR PERFORMANCE LOOP RESET.....................................45
    PERVERSION LOOP RESET..46
    PRIDE LOOP RESET..47

REBELLION LOOP RESET	48
REJECTION LOOP RESET	49
SELF-HATRED LOOP RESET	50
SHAME LOOP RESET	51
SUPPRESSED ANGER LOOP RESET	52
TRAUMA LOOP RESET	53
VICTIM LOOP RESET	54

Part 3: Breaking Free 55

THE FREEDOM FRAMEWORK: 57
GOING FROM THE FRUIT TO THE ROOT 57
STEP 1. FIND THE SNARE(S) 57
STEP 2. TRACE THE DESTRUCTIVE LOOP 58
STEP 3. CALL IT OUT 62
STEP 4. SEE IT EVERYWHERE 62
STEP 5. DIG TO THE ROOT 63
STEP 6: STEPPING INTO FREEDOM 65

Part 4: Resources for Leaders 71

Leader's Guide Cheat Sheet 73
26 Destructive Loop Overview 74
Quick Reference Index 79
A Case Study: Dismantling the Snares of Addiction, Perversion, and Perfectionism 83
A Second Case Study: Dismantling the Snares of Perfectionism, Shame, and Suppressed Anger 87

Living in and From Freedom 91

Frequently Asked Questions 93

About This Resource 93
About Deliverance & Spiritual Warfare 93
About Therapy & Professional Care 94
Practical Application 95
For Leaders & Ministry Use 96
About Declarations & Renewing the Mind 96
Troubleshooting 97
Final Encouragement 98

Glossary 99

Other Resources 107

About the Author 109

Preface

"...let us throw off everything that hinders and the sin that so easily entangles. And let us run with perseverance the race marked out for us..." - Hebrews 12:1

The Problem This Book Seeks to Address

What if freedom wasn't just a moment at an altar or at the end of a ministry session, but a daily reality? What if the cycles that have gripped you for years could be dismantled with simple, Spirit-led steps? You weren't made to white-knuckle your way through sanctification. You were made to walk in the supernatural power of a God who not only sets you free but equips you to stay free.

It's one thing to cast a demon out. It's another thing to tear down the pattern of thought and stronghold of belief that was built in partnership with it. It's yet another thing altogether to then replace that stronghold so that the strongman demon doesn't have anything to come back to.

This book provides tools to help identify the strongholds many people still face after deliverance or as they go through their deliverance journey. Strongholds are patterns of thought built IN PARTNERSHIP with demons. Even after the demon leaves, the patterns often remain. This book helps you dismantle those patterns so the enemy has nothing to return to (Matthew 12:43-45).

We aim to equip you to live free, not just get free.

I'm tired of seeing the people of God get their teeth kicked in and legs cut out from under them by destructive patterns in their lives. I'm also tired of seeing people tolerate and accept things that don't have to be a part of their lives. I'm especially tired of the church not always realizing that's happening.

If you're weary, stuck, or simply hungry for more of God, you're in the right place. This book was birthed out of necessity in living rooms, prayer retreats, and deliverance sessions—places where hungry people gathered to encounter a living God who has the power to set them free. It was in those places that many people learned to hear God's voice and discovered that freedom grows through simple, repeatable steps toward the Father, empowered by the Holy Spirit and made possible by Jesus.

A point of clarification - Throughout this book, we use 'loop,' 'stronghold,' 'pattern,' and 'snare' interchangeably—they all refer to the same thing: a destructive cycle that keeps you stuck.

Other Tensions For Why This Book Is Necessary

For years, I've watched people who genuinely love Jesus but are stuck in cycles they can't seem to break: fear that spirals into control, shame that fuels secrecy, rejection that breeds perfectionism, and numbness that quiets the heart in worship. Most of us don't wake up wanting to be in bondage; instead, we drift into agreements that feel true in the moment and then wonder why we feel far from God.

At the same time, many churches want a biblical, safe way to practice deliverance that is part of the natural disciple-making journey. They aren't looking for extremes or theatrics. That's the gap this book aims to fill. **Undoing the Enemy's Snares** offers clear language, simple prayers, anchoring Scripture, and small next steps you can take on your discipleship journey before, during, and after your deliverance. The hope is that you can cooperate with the Holy Spirit in everyday life. Think of this as a diagnostic map and a guide for walking with Jesus into lasting freedom.

Who I Am and How I Came To This Work

I'm a Holy Spirit–filled pastor who has spent years serving the local church and the wider Body of Christ through a deliverance and healing ministry with The Defining Place.

I've authored material such as **Deliverance Demystified: Unlocking Biblical Answers to Real Questions for Lasting Freedom** and *The Deliverance and Inner Healing Manual: A Spirit-Empowered Guide to Unlocking Biblical Freedom and Wholeness*. I've also served in church planting, in leadership at local Adult & Teen Challenges, and now back in pastoral ministry at a local church, where my heart beats to see people encounter God's love and be equipped to live free.

My greatest desire is to help others encounter the Living God and be restored to intimacy with Him. I want everyone to hear the voice of God, learn to live free, and carry His kingdom into a world that needs Him.

My Philosophy

When I think of a model to follow, I think of Jesus' example. He only did what he saw the Father doing and only said what he heard the Father saying. I figure if I'm to follow Jesus, then that should be my model for life and ministry, too. Along the way, I've learned that it is helpful for many to lay out some fence posts. For instance, everything we do should be:

- Rooted in Scripture
- Led by the Holy Spirit
- Ministered with the heart of a shepherd
- Spoken boldly

Only when we partner with what God is saying and doing will we experience lasting breakthrough.

Let Me Be Clear About Therapy and Medicine's Role

I am not opposed to therapy or medicine.

I am grateful for wise medical and mental-health partners. In fact, I bless integrated care and encourage it when needed. Deliverance and discipleship belong in the lives of the people of God.

Both deliverance and discipleship work well with wise counseling, good medicine, and healthy community.

What I mean by "deliverance" (and what I don't mean)

By "deliverance," I mean partnering with Jesus to identify and remove anything that has slowed us down or has entangled us. In practice, that means breaking agreements with lies and sin, closing doors to the demonic, removing the influence of demons from our lives, and learning to live in God's truth. It looks like repentance, forgiveness, renunciation, and the renewal of the mind. It sounds like short, sincere prayers and commands infused with the power and Spirit of the living God. All of it is made possible by the death, burial, and resurrection of Jesus Christ.

Deliverance produces fruit like peace, purity, and love. It is to be done in conjunction with discipleship, not as a shortcut around discipleship. Deliverance often catalyzes growth alongside wise counseling and medical care.

Who This Resource Is For

- **Individuals** who love Jesus and are tired of feeling hijacked by the same unhealthy reactions.
- **Small groups** that want a safe, simple way to walk together in greater freedom.
- **Pastors and leaders** who need something reproducible in prayer rooms, teams, and one-to-one settings.
- **Intercessors** who want language that aligns prayer with Scripture and the Father's heart while exposing the schemes of the enemy.

If you're skeptical, you're welcome here. You don't have to agree with everything in order to try a simple prayer and see what happens. If past excesses or extremes have wounded you, I'm sorry. This book is designed to be calm, clear, and safe. If you're ready to take a positive step in your walk with the Lord, start by identifying and breaking the unhealthy cycles and patterns in your life. Use the loops on the following pages to focus on the ones that appear most frequently.

Jesus will meet you there.

You're Not Meant to Stay Stuck

The enemy loves to convince God's people that the cycle they're in is just "how they are." That the pattern is permanent, that freedom is for everyone else but not for them. That's a lie.

You were made for more than managing sin—you were made for walking in victory. The tools in the pages ahead aren't complex or mystical. They're simple, biblical, and Spirit-empowered.

And they work. Not because they're brilliant, but because the finished work of Jesus Christ is sufficient for every snare the enemy sets. Let's get you untangled.

Introduction

Before You Begin

Before we jump into the 5-Minute RESET or the 26 loops, you need to understand how the enemy operates. Snares don't appear out of nowhere—they're built. Step by step. Thought by thought. Agreement by agreement.

The good news? What's been built can be dismantled.

In the following few pages, you'll see precisely how a wound becomes a stronghold and why catching it early changes everything. This is the foundation for everything that follows.

Read slowly. Ask the Holy Spirit to show you what's really been happening and then to help you break free.

Tools to Help You Exit The Destructive Patterns You're Stuck In

Everything in the following pages is meant to be a practical tool for freedom and growth.

Each tool is simple enough to use on its own and strong enough to use with a trusted friend, a small group, or a ministry leader. Think of each tool as a companion to your walk with Jesus and, when needed, with professional care.

Below, we've laid out how to RESET from a loop, pattern, cycle, or stronghold (we use those terms interchangeably) and quickly exit the destructive pattern you've been caught in.

When To Use These Tools:

- When you recognize a destructive pattern but haven't yet had deliverance
- As a part of your deliverance journey to get to the root of issues faster
- After deliverance, when you notice old patterns returning
- When you've been delivered but still struggle with certain thoughts/behaviors
- As part of ongoing discipleship and disciplemaking relationships
- As a way to take inventory of your life and renew your mind
- In small groups for mutual accountability

NOTE: This tool complements deliverance ministry but doesn't replace it. If you suspect you need deliverance and haven't gone through it yet, schedule a session with a trained minister. If you have questions about what deliverance is or how it might apply to your life, then start with ***Deliverance Demystified***.

WHAT IF I SEE MULTIPLE LOOPS?

It's common to identify 2-4 interconnected loops. Here's what to do:

1. Identify which loop is MOST ACTIVE right now
2. Start there - breaking one often loosens others
3. Notice how loops "feed" each other (e.g., Rejection → Perfectionism → Shame)
4. Address them one at a time, but be aware of the connections
5. Use the "See It Everywhere" step to map how they interact
6. See the case studies (p. 83, 87) for examples of addressing multiple loops.

Using These Tools Alone

1. Start with prayer - invite the Holy Spirit to guide you
2. Read through the Quick Reference Index (p. 79) and identify which loop feels most familiar
3. Use the 5-Minute RESET first - don't jump to the 6-step process immediately
4. Work through ONE loop at a time (even if you see multiple)
5. Consider sharing your findings with a trusted friend, mentor, or pastor
6. Remember: Freedom is a journey, not a one-time event

Understanding Snares:
How Destructive Patterns and Strongholds Form

"They promise them freedom, while they themselves are slaves of depravity—for 'people are slaves to whatever has mastered them.'" 2 Peter 2:19

We are engaged in a spiritual battle — one that often plays out not just in big, visible struggles, but also in subtle, repeating patterns deep within our hearts and minds.

Without even realizing it, we can find ourselves trapped in *emotional and spiritual loops*: cycles of thought, feeling, and behavior that steal our freedom, distort our identity, and hinder our relationship with God and others. These loops are not random; they are part of the enemy's strategy to keep us isolated, wounded, and ineffective.

The Destructive Loop: How a Wound Becomes a Stronghold

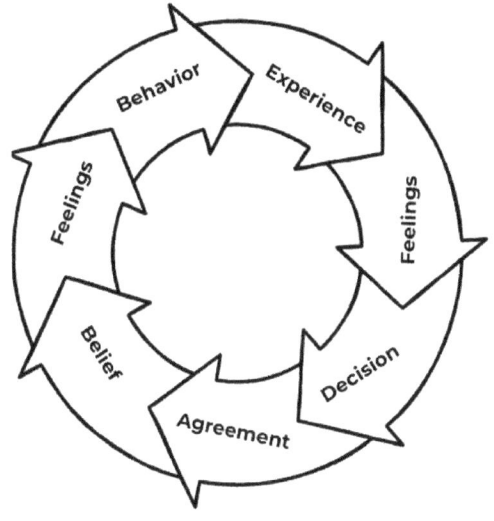

→ An event or **Experience** Causes certain **Feelings**

→ Those feelings lead to a **Decision**

→ That decision forms an **Agreement** in the spiritual realm

→ Those agreements reinforce **Belief(s)**

→ Those beliefs lead to other **Feelings and Behaviors**

→ Those **Behavior(s)** create new **Experience(s)** that reinforce the original **Beliefs**.

If we don't end the cycle, eventually those experiences compound and leave a wake of destruction. The **good news is that we are not powerless**. Through the finished work of Jesus Christ, we have been given the authority to recognize, resist, and break free from every plan of the enemy.

The 5 Minute RESET Quickstart

When you feel stuck, overwhelmed, or tempted—use this fast track.

- **R — Recognize the loop**
  Read the "Pattern" and "How it feels" sections. Name what's happening.
- **E — Expose the agreements**
  Write one sentence you've been believing or saying that isn't from God.
- **S — Submit to Jesus**
  Pray a short prayer of repentance and forgiveness (as needed).
- **E — Exchange lies for truth**
  Choose one or two 'I Am' or 'God Is' statements and declare them aloud daily to renew your mind.
- **T — Take a next step**
  Do one "Interrupt Step" immediately. Tell a safe person if you need support.

In the following pages, we have laid out our recommended six steps to get free or to help set others free from the destructive patterns in your life.

A Full Session Consists of 6 Steps

GET SET FREE

6 Steps to Dismantling and Escaping the Snares of the Enemy

1. FEEL THE SNARE

ASK: What's tripping me up?
Where do you feel stuck?
What keeps showing up?

Psalm 139:23–24; Romans 7:19

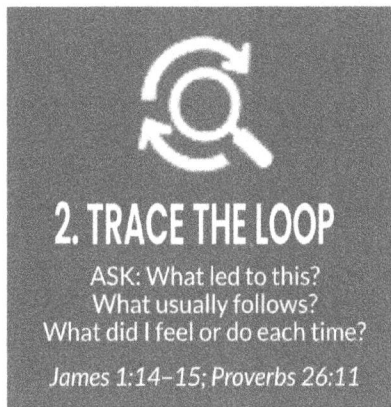

2. TRACE THE LOOP

ASK: What led to this?
What usually follows?
What did I feel or do each time?

James 1:14–15; Proverbs 26:11

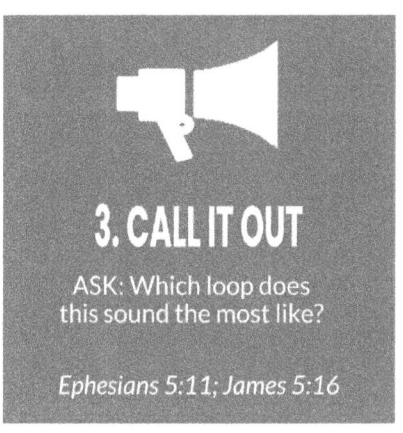

3. CALL IT OUT

ASK: Which loop does this sound the most like?

Ephesians 5:11; James 5:16

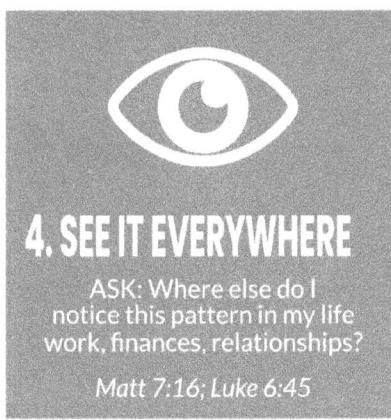

4. SEE IT EVERYWHERE

ASK: Where else do I notice this pattern in my life work, finances, relationships?

Matt 7:16; Luke 6:45

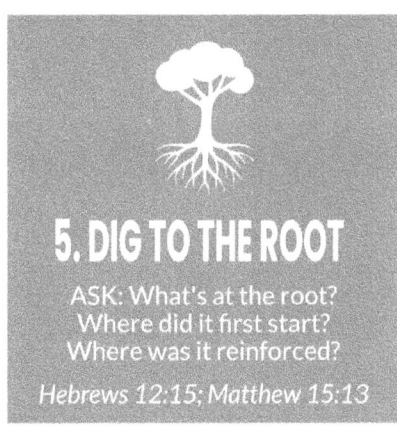

5. DIG TO THE ROOT

ASK: What's at the root?
Where did it first start?
Where was it reinforced?

Hebrews 12:15; Matthew 15:13

6. STEP INTO FREEDOM

- Renounce • Repent
- Forgive • Replace
- Declare • Live it

2 Corinthians 5:17; Romans 12:1–2

...let us throw off everything that hinders and the sin that so easily entangles. And let us run with perseverance the race marked out for us, fixing our eyes on Jesus... Hebrews 12:1-2

How to Use This Guide

This guide exposes 26 of the most common destructive loops/cycles/strongholds or patterns of belief or behavior that the enemy uses to keep people bound.

- **Pray First** - Before you begin, ask the Holy Spirit to reveal any loops that may be active in your life or in the lives of those you are ministering to.

- **Read Slowly and Reflectively** - Don't rush through the loops. As you read each one, pause and allow the Lord to highlight anything that resonates with your personal experience.

- **Recognize and Name the Pattern** - If you see a loop that feels familiar, that's great. Awareness is the first step toward freedom.

- **Understand the Progression** – Ignoring a moment of pain, fear, abuse, or offense doesn't stop the loop. Instead, it accelerates it. The earlier you respond to the Holy Spirit's promptings and process what's happening in the moment, the easier it is to break free and stay on the path to life.

- **One Loop Can Easily Lead Into Another** - Picture the loops like connected highways. If you don't exit a destructive pattern early, you can quickly speed into another one without even realizing it. Fear can feed control, anger can fuel shame, and rejection can spiral into bitterness. Recognizing where you are gives you a chance to exit the highway before you get deeper into bondage or before the highway leads you to destruction.

- **Repent, Renounce, and Receive** - Confess any agreements you've made with these patterns. Renounce them. Receive God's truth and healing in their place.

- **Respond Actively** - Journal what God reveals. Pray through specific areas of pain, bitterness, or bondage. Make intentional decisions about how you will interrupt the loops. If needed, reach out to trusted prayer partners, leaders, or pastors for support or deliverance.

- **Interrupt the Loop & Choose a New Path** - Freedom comes not just by breaking old patterns, but by actively choosing new, life-giving ones. Ask the Holy Spirit, *"What's a way of responding that leads to life rather than death?"* Then take a step of obedience and walk it out. Breaking free isn't just about resisting — it's about replacing the old pattern with a new, Spirit-led response. For example:

    - Instead of withdrawing, reach out to someone you trust (for real impact, decide who you will reach out to and what you'll do if they don't respond).

    - Instead of staying silent in fear, declare the truth of who you are aloud, wherever you are. Instead of holding on to bitterness, release forgiveness immediately and fully. These steps of faith disrupt the enemy's schemes and create new patterns of freedom.

- **Revisit as Needed** - Remember, healing often happens in layers. Return to this guide as the Holy Spirit leads, using it as a tool for deeper freedom & transformation over time.
- **My prayer is** that this resource will open your eyes, stir your heart, and empower you to move from bondage into lasting freedom.

Choosing Where To Start
- Begin with the loop you feel most often (e.g., perfectionism / performance is one of the loops we see most often because it is born out of rejection or fear). Other major loops are control, overwhelm, perversion, anger, fear, addiction, and numbness.
- Loops can **overlap**. If another loop lights up while you work, finish the one you're on, then address the next one in a future session.

Using This With a Friend or Leader
- **Posture**: gentle, curious, non-rushed. Ask short, open questions.
- **Boundaries**: minister in pairs when possible; honor confidentiality; avoid cross-gender 1:1 in private settings.
- **Flow**: read the loop, listen for agreements, pray short prayers, speak truth, choose one simple step, and schedule a check-in.

Using this in a Small Group
- Keep stories brief and appropriate and avoid graphic details.
- Do a shared practice: everyone selects a loop, journals quietly, then (optionally) pairs to pray declarations over one another.
- Close with thanksgiving and one specific next step per person.

Daily & Weekly Rhythm
- **Daily** (3–5 min):
  - Use the **RESET** quickstart + one declaration you carry all day.
  - Use the **Morning Check-in (page 65)** and **Evening Check-in (page 66)** worksheets daily.
- **Weekly** (20–30 min):
  - Complete a whole session on the loop that is most active that week.
  - Use the **30 Day Tracker (page 67)**
- **Monthly**: Review your notes. Notice patterns. Celebrate progress.

I Am Declarations
- Choose one or two primary "I Am" or "God Is" statements related to your main loop. Write them on an index card to carry or post where visible.
- Memorize the associated scriptures.

When You Feel Stuck

- Go slower. Speak declarations out loud. Ask someone to pray with you.
- If strong emotions, trauma memories, or safety concerns surface, pause and follow the guidance in the [Pastoral Acknowledgment & Safety Note](#).

A Word of Encouragement

Freedom grows with:

- Courageous honesty
- Practical humility
- Healthy community
- Discipleship
- Continual practice

Jesus is gentle and powerful. Let Him lead as you take the next small step. Allow Him to lead you into lasting change.

Key Scriptures For Freedom

Declare them aloud daily to renew your mind.

- "For he has rescued us from the dominion of darkness and brought us into the kingdom of the Son he loves." Colossian 1:13

- "May God himself, the God of peace, sanctify you through and through. May your whole spirit, soul, and body be kept blameless at the coming of our Lord Jesus Christ." 1 Thess 5:23

- "But because of his great love for us, God, who is rich in mercy, made us alive with Christ even when we were dead in transgressions. It is by grace you have been saved." Eph 2:4–5

- "And you also were included in Christ when you heard the message of truth, the gospel of your salvation. When you believed, you were marked in him with a seal, the promised Holy Spirit." Eph 1:13

- "He heals the brokenhearted and binds up their wounds." Psalm 147:3

- "...so that Satan might not outwit us. For we are not unaware of his schemes." 2 Cor 2:11

- "The weapons we fight with are not the weapons of the world. On the contrary, they have divine power to demolish strongholds. We demolish arguments and every pretension that sets itself up against the knowledge of God," 2 Cor 10:4-5

- "The reason the Son of God appeared was to destroy the devil's work." 1 John 3:8

- "Do not conform to the pattern of this world, but be transformed by the renewing of your mind." Rom 12:2

- "It is for freedom that Christ has set us free." Gal 5:1

- "People are slaves to whatever has mastered them." 2 Pet 2:19

- "He has sent me to bind up the brokenhearted, to proclaim freedom for the captives..." Isa 61:1

A Final Reminder Before Beginning

You were made for freedom.
Don't settle for patterns of destruction.
Stand in the victory Jesus has already won!

Part 2: Detailed Examination of the 26 Destructive Loops

You're about to encounter 26 patterns the enemy uses to keep God's people bound. Some will feel uncomfortably familiar. Others might surprise you. As you read, ask the Holy Spirit: "*Which loop is most active in my life right now?*"

Let Him highlight the one or two that matter most in this season. Start there.

Freedom grows when we're honest about where we're stuck and courageously obedient to take the next step. The enemy will want you to feel overwhelmed by how many loops there are. God wants you to see hope in how clearly each one can be dismantled.

Remember, this is meant to be a map to freedom, not a list of problems or excuses.

OVERVIEW OF THE ENEMY'S 26 DESTRUCTIVE LOOPS

1. Abandonment Loop
Abandonment → Fear of Being Alone → Anxiety → Clinging or Walls → Control → Disconnection → Rejection (Real or Perceived) → Offense → Unforgiveness → Hopelessness → Destruction

2. Accusation Loop
Pain or Insecurity → Fault-Finding → Gossip/Slander → Division → Guilt → Self-Righteousness → Blindness to Own Sin → Hardness of Heart → Defensiveness → Isolation → Rejection (real or perceived) → Accusation (of self or others) → Destruction

3. Addiction Loop
Pain → Escape → Temporary Relief → Guilt → Shame → Hiding → Craving → Relapse → Destruction

4. Anger Loop
Anger → Offense → Unforgiveness → Bitterness → Hatred → Vengeance → Murderous Thoughts → Destruction

5. Apathy Loop
Disappointment → Disengagement → Numbness → Lack of Motivation → Hopelessness → Inaction → Missed Purpose → Destruction

6. Betrayal Loop
Trust → Betrayal → Shock → Anger → Vows or Walls → Bitterness → Distrust → Isolation → Destruction

7. Bitterness Loop
Offense → Unforgiveness → Bitterness → Justification → Hardness of Heart → Isolation → Deception → Spiritual Blindness → Destruction

8. Comparison Loop
Insecurity → Comparison → Jealousy or Self-Rejection → Striving or Sabotage → Resentment → Bitterness → Shame or Pride → Destruction

9. Control Loop
Control → Disconnection → Rejection (Real or Perceived) → Offense → Unforgiveness → Hopelessness → Destruction

10. Fear Loop
Fear → Anxiety → Catastrophizing → Hesitation → Withdrawal → Missed Opportunity → Blame → Condemnation → Hopelessness → Paralysis → Destruction

11. Grief Loop
Grief → Numbness → Withdrawal → Suppression → Anger → Bitterness → Hopelessness → Death Agreements → Destruction

12. Identity Confusion Loop
Accusation / Lack of Affirmation → Confusion → People-Pleasing → Compromise → Regret → Shame → Self-Rejection → Despair → Destruction

13. Idolatry Loop
Discontent → Idol or Substitute Source → Temporary Relief → Attachment → Guilt → Spiritual Numbness → Hardness of Heart → Destruction

14. Isolation Loop
Pain or Disappointment → Withdrawal → Distrust → Self-Protection → Lack of Community → Loneliness → Despair → Destruction

15. Numbness Loop
Pain or Overwhelm → Emotional Numbness → Disengagement → Passivity → Isolation → Depression → Hopelessness → Destruction

16. Overwhelm Loop
Overwhelm → Anxiety → Control or Paralysis → Exhaustion → Despair → Hopelessness → Destruction

17. Perfectionism or Performance
Rejection (often through correction) → Pressure → Fear (of failure and further rejection) → Desire for Control → Lack of Trust → Overworking or Perfectionism → Exhaustion → Shame → Self Condemnation → Burnout → Destruction

18. Perversion Loop
Wound or Exposure → Curiosity → Indulgence → Guilt → Shame → Secrecy → Craving → Escalation → Destruction

19. Pride Loop
Pride → Independence → Refusal to Receive Help → Rejection of Others → Isolation → Frustration → Stagnation → Judgment of Others → Fall/Failure → Shame → Self-Hatred → Destruction

20. Rebellion Loop
Wounding or Control by Others → Rebellion → Independence → Justification → Deception → Isolation → Sin Patterns → Hardness of Heart → Destruction

21. Rejection Loop
Rejection → Insecurity → Comparison → Self-Rejection → Isolation → Bitterness → Hatred → Destruction

22. Self-Hatred Loop
Abuse, Wound, or Rejection → Offense → Fear → Negative Self-Talk → Comparison → Self Rejection → Disgust → Shame → Despair → Self-Blame → Destructive Behaviors → Reinforced Self-Hatred → Destruction

23. Shame Loop
Shame → Fear of Rejection → Hiding → Accusation → Self-Imposed Rejection → Control/Perfectionism → Exhaustion or Breakdown → Destruction

24. Suppressed Anger Loop
Anger → Silence/Suppression → Resentment → Guilt → Shame → Self-Accusation → Depression → Physical Symptoms (sickness, fatigue) → Breakdown → Destruction

25. Trauma Loop
Trauma → Fear → Hyper-vigilance → Isolation → Emotional Numbness → Disconnection → Despair → Destruction

26. Victim Loop
Injustice → Pain → Defensiveness → Offense → Justification → Blame → Powerlessness → Entitlement → Pride → Destruction

ABANDONMENT LOOP RESET

Destructive Pattern:

Abandonment → Fear of Being Alone → Anxiety → Clinging or Walls → Control → Disconnection → Rejection (Real or Perceived) → Offense → Unforgiveness → Hopelessness → Destruction

Often Triggered By:

Real, Perceived, or Threat of Loss

How This Loop May Feel in Real Life:

Someone important leaves physically or emotionally → A deep fear rises that you will always be alone → Anxiety begins to hum in the background → This anxiety and fear causes you to either cling too tightly to people or build walls to protect yourself → All of these actions leads to attempting to control relationships → Those attempts eventually push people away leaving you feeling disconnected → The distance confirms your fears → You interpret this as rejection, which fuels offense and unforgiveness → Hope for close, safe relationships fades and you begin to abandon others before they could do that to you.

Declarations (with Scripture):

- God will never leave me or forsake me. (Hebrews 13:5)
- I am not an orphan—I am a child of God. (John 14:18; Romans 8:15)
- I am never truly alone. (Matthew 28:20)
- God places the lonely in families. (Psalm 68:6)
- My security is found in Christ, not in people. (Colossians 3:3)

Sample Prayer:

Father, I confess the pain of feeling abandoned. I repent for building walls or grasping for people out of fear. I renounce every lie that says I'm alone or unwanted. I receive Your faithful love and presence. Anchor me in Your nearness, and teach me to love with healthy trust.

Journal Prompts:

- Where did I first feel abandoned, and what did I believe?
- How have I guarded my heart in fear of being alone?
- What does God's presence say to that fear?

Steps that Interrupt the Abandonment Loop:

- Bring the Pain to God — Acknowledge the wound of abandonment and give it to God.
- Anchor Yourself — Receive the truth that God will never leave you.
- Release Control — Stop clinging or walling off, and surrender relationships to God.
- Choose Connection — Open your heart to safe people and pursue healthy bonds.
- Forgive Freely — Release those who left or rejected you into God's hands.
- Live Secure in Love — Walk forward with hope, knowing you are never truly alone.

See Also: Control, Grief, Isolation, Performance, Rejection

ACCUSATION LOOP RESET

Destructive Pattern:
Pain or Insecurity → Fault-Finding → Gossip/Slander → Division → Guilt → Self-Righteousness → Blindness to Own Sin → Hardness of Heart → Defensiveness → Isolation → Rejection (real or perceived) → Accusation (of self or others) → Destruction

Often Triggered By:
Pain, Hurt Feelings, Being Overlooked, Slander

How This Loop May Feel in Real Life:
You feel hurt, overlooked, or insecure → Instead of addressing the wound, you start focusing on others' faults or your own → Conversations shift into gossip, criticism, or slander → Relationships strain and division grows → Deep down you feel guilt, but pride frames it as "righteous" judgment → This blinds you to your own faults → Your heart hardens toward correction and toward others because "they just don't get you" → You grow defensive and isolate yourself → Isolation fuels feelings of rejection → The cycle continues with accusations toward others or yourself, leaving you empty and hopeless.

Declarations (with Scripture):
- I use my words to build up, not tear down. (Ephesians 4:29)
- I walk in humility and seek peace. (Romans 12:18; Philippians 2:3)
- I confess my sins and receive grace. (1 John 1:9)
- I choose unity over judgment. (Psalm 133:1)
- I overcome the accuser by the blood of the Lamb. (Revelation 12:10–11)

Sample Prayer:
God, I repent for judging others and using my words to divide instead of heal. I renounce the spirit of accusation and every agreement with pride and fault-finding. I receive Your grace and truth. Help me speak life, walk in humility, and build unity in the body of Christ.

Journal Prompts:
- Where have I criticized or judged instead of encouraged?
- What insecurity might be driving my need to accuse?
- How can I speak life today?

Steps that Interrupt the Accusation Loop:
- Bring the Hurt to God — Be honest about your pain instead of projecting it on others.
- Choose Humility — Let God reveal your own heart before judging someone else's.
- Guard Your Words — Refuse gossip, criticism, and slander; speak life instead.
- Pursue Peace — Seek reconciliation and unity where possible.
- Stay Teachable — Receive correction with grace and keep your heart soft.
- Walk in Love and Truth — Replace accusation with encouragement and connection.

See Also: Anger, Bitterness, Perversion, Pride, Shame, Suppressed Anger

ADDICTION LOOP RESET

Destructive Pattern:

Pain → Escape → Temporary Relief → Guilt → Shame → Hiding → Craving → Relapse → Destruction

Often Triggered By:

Pain, Stress, Overwhelm, Need for Pleasure

How This Loop May Feel in Real Life:

You feel pain, stress, or emptiness that feels too heavy to carry → To escape, you turn to a behavior or substance that brings quick relief → For a moment, it numbs the pain and feels like control is restored → Soon after, guilt creeps in, and you wonder why you gave in again → Shame deepens, convincing you that you'll never be free → To hide the struggle, you withdraw from others and pretend you're okay → Isolation intensifies the cravings, pulling you back toward the same escape → The cycle repeats with relapse, leaving you feeling defeated and trapped.

Declarations (with Scripture):

- I am no longer a slave to sin. (Romans 6:6-7)
- I take every thought captive to Christ. (2 Corinthians 10:5)
- God is my refuge and comfort. (Psalm 46:1; 2 Corinthians 1:3–4)
- I am free through the Spirit of the Lord. (2 Corinthians 3:17)
- I live by the Spirit, not by the flesh. (Galatians 5:16)

Sample Prayer:

Jesus, I bring my pain and broken patterns to You. I repent for turning to false comforts instead of trusting You. I renounce addiction and every spirit of escape, lust, or bondage. Cleanse me and fill me with Your Spirit. Help me renew my mind and walk in true freedom.

Journal Prompts:

- What am I using to escape pain?
- What truth does God offer instead?
- Who can walk with me in accountability?

Steps that Interrupt the Addiction Loop:

- Give the Pain to God — Bring your hurt honestly to Him instead of escaping it.
- Seek Healthy Comfort — Replace false escapes with practices and relationships.
- Confess, Forgive, and Release Guilt — Walk in forgiveness through Christ.
- Break Agreement with Shame — Declare your identity as loved and accepted, not defined by failure. Live in Community — Invite trusted people into your journey so you don't hide.
- Build New Disciplines — Scripture, prayer, and renewed habits.

See Also: Isolation, Numbness, Overwhelm, Performance, Perversion, Pride, Shame, Anger

ANGER LOOP RESET

Destructive Pattern:
Anger → Offense → Unforgiveness → Bitterness → Hatred → Vengeance → Murderous Thoughts → Destruction

Often Triggered By:
Offense, Grief, Jealousy

How This Loop May Feel in Real Life:
Someone offends you—maybe through words, betrayal, or disrespect → Instead of processing it, you hold on tightly to the offense and replay it in your mind → The wound deepens into unforgiveness, and you feel justified in keeping the person "in debt" where they owe you → Over time, bitterness seeps in, coloring how you see that person and even others → The bitterness hardens into hatred—you no longer just dislike them, you feel a burning against them → Thoughts of revenge or wishing them harm rise, even if you don't act on them → Left unchecked, these feelings fuel destructive fantasies or murderous thoughts that scare you or harden you further → What started as a wound ends with destruction, leaving you isolated, guilty, and trapped in anger's grip.

Declarations (with Scripture):
- I am slow to anger and abounding in love. (James 1:19-20; Psalm 103:8)
- I forgive as Christ has forgiven me. (Colossians 3:13)
- I release the offense and trust God to make things right. (Romans 12:19)
- The peace of Christ rules in my heart. (Colossians 3:15)
- I am filled with compassion, not resentment. (Ephesians 4:31-32)

Sample Prayer:
Father, I bring my pain and anger before You. I repent for holding onto offense and unforgiveness. I renounce bitterness and every desire for revenge. I choose to forgive fully and trust You as my defender. Fill me with Your peace and teach me to walk in mercy.

Journal Prompts:
- What hurt have I been holding onto?
- Who do I need to release to God today?
- What does walking in peace look like in this relationship?

Steps that Interrupt the Anger Loop:
- Name the Hurt Honestly — Acknowledge where the offense pierced you.
- Release the Offense and Pain — Refuse to replay or nurse it; place it in God's hands.
- Forgive from the Heart — Choose forgiveness, even before you feel it.
- Invite God's Justice — Trust Him as defender instead of seeking revenge.
- Receive His Compassion — Let His mercy soften your bitterness.
- Walk in Peace — Take intentional steps to extend grace and respond with love.

See Also: Betrayal, Bitterness, Control, Numbness, Overwhelm, Performance, Perversion, Pride, Shame, Suppressed Anger, Victim

APATHY LOOP RESET

Destructive Pattern:

Disappointment → Disengagement → Numbness → Lack of Motivation → Hopelessness → Inaction → Missed Purpose → Destruction

Often Triggered By:

Disappointment, Fear, Pain, Rejection

How This Loop May Feel in Real Life

You face a disappointment or setback that shakes your expectations → Instead of pressing through, you start to pull back emotionally and mentally → Life begins to feel dull or flat, and you lose the drive to engage → Motivation fades, and even small tasks feel too heavy to start or finish → History proves everything is pointless, and your vision for more dims → Days begin to pass without forward movement, and opportunities slip by → The lack of action reinforces the belief that nothing will change, keeping you stuck and missing the very purpose you were made for.

Declarations (with Scripture):

- The joy of the Lord is my strength. (Nehemiah 8:10)
- God is doing a new thing in me. (Isaiah 43:19)
- I am not lazy but fervent in spirit. (Romans 12:11)
- I will not grow weary in doing good. (Galatians 6:9)
- God has good works prepared for me. (Ephesians 2:10)

Sample Prayer:

Father, I repent for growing numb and disengaged. I've allowed disappointment to deaden my desire. I renounce apathy and every spirit of sloth, despair, or indifference. Reignite my heart with purpose and joy. Help me take the next step in partnership with Your Spirit.

Journal Prompts:

- What disappointment triggered this disengagement?
- What's one area where God wants to rekindle vision?
- What small step can I take today?

Steps that Interrupt the Apathy Loop:

- Grieve Honestly — Allow yourself to feel the loss so it doesn't harden your heart.
- Reignite Passion — Ask God to stir fresh desire and restore joy within you.
- Take Small, Faithful Steps — Become unstuck by choosing simple acts of obedience.
- Rediscover God's Vision — Fix your eyes on God's purposes instead of past setbacks.
- Partner with the Holy Spirit Daily — Depend on His strength, not your own.
- Live Intentionally with Joy — Embrace each day as a chance to bear fruit in hope.

See Also: Grief, Isolation, Overwhelm, Numbness

BETRAYAL LOOP RESET

Destructive Pattern:
Misplaced or Broken Trust → Betrayal → Shock → Anger → Vows or Walls → Bitterness → Distrust → Isolation → Destruction

Often Triggered By:
Deception, Offense, Wounding

How This Loop May Feel in Real Life:
You place your trust in someone and feel safe → That trust is broken through betrayal or deception → You feel shocked, wounded, and deeply angry → To protect yourself, you make inner vows or build emotional walls, promising never to let it happen again → Bitterness grows when the hurt isn't acknowledged or the relationship isn't restored → Fear convinces you that others will act the same way, making trust feel impossible → Over time, you pull away from one relationship after another, severing connections and living in isolation → The wound travels with you, quietly shaping how you see every relationship and situation.

Declarations (with Scripture):
- The Lord is close to the brokenhearted and saves the crushed in spirit. (Psalm 34:18)
- I choose to forgive as Christ forgave me. (Colossians 3:13)
- I trust God to heal every wound and rebuild trust. (Jeremiah 30:17)
- I will not live behind walls—I am safe in God. (Proverbs 18:10)
- I release bitterness and walk in peace. (Hebrews 12:14–15)

Sample Prayer:
Father, I bring You the betrayal that wounded me. I repent for building walls and making inner vows to protect myself. I forgive those who hurt me and release them to You. I renounce bitterness and mistrust. Heal my heart and teach me to walk in love and safety again.

Journal Prompts:
- What vows or inner defenses have I made because of betrayal?
- What would it look like to forgive fully and walk free?
- Where is God inviting me to risk connection again?

Steps that Interrupt the Betrayal Loop:
- Grieve the Betrayal — Acknowledge and process the pain honestly.
- Invite God's Healing — Let Him touch the deepest places of the wound.
- Forgive with His Strength — Release the offender to God's justice.
- Tear Down Inner Vows — Let go of self-protection that blocks love.
- Let Go of Bitterness — Choose freedom over resentment.
- Learn to Trust Again — Re-engage in safe, healthy relationships.

See Also: Anger, Bitterness, Grief, Isolation, Overwhelm, Numbness, Rejection

BITTERNESS LOOP RESET

Destructive Pattern:

Offense → Unforgiveness → Bitterness → Justification → Hardness of Heart → Isolation → Deception → Spiritual Blindness → Destruction

Often Triggered By:

Offense, Hurt, Betrayal, Criticism

How This Loop May Feel in Real Life:

Someone hurts you, betrays you, or says something offensive → You hold onto the offense instead of processing it with God → Unforgiveness sets in, and bitterness begins to grow → You start justifying your resentment, replaying the hurt over and over → Your heart hardens, making it difficult to receive love or correction → You pull away from people or at least that person, convinced you're protecting yourself → Over time, lies twist your perspective, making it harder to see truth or trust God fully → Eventually, the hope of any relationship or restoration of one is destroyed.

Declarations (with Scripture):

- I guard my heart against bitterness. (Hebrews 12:15)
- I forgive as I have been forgiven. (Ephesians 4:32)
- I keep my heart soft and open to God. (Ezekiel 36:26)
- I walk in the light and truth. (1 John 1:7)
- I entrust justice to the Lord. (Romans 12:19)

Sample Prayer:

Jesus, I confess the bitterness I've been carrying. I repent of my unforgiveness, isolation, and for hardening my heart. I renounce every lie that says I have the right to stay offended. I choose to forgive and release, to live with a soft heart and trust You with justice.

Journal Prompts:

- Who am I still holding bitterness toward?
- How has that bitterness affected my heart and relationships?
- What would walking in forgiveness look like this week?

Steps that Interrupt the Bitterness Loop:

- Acknowledge the Wound — Bring the hurt into God's light instead of hiding it.
- Release the Offense to God — Let go of the need to hold it or replay it.
- Choose Forgiveness Daily — Even if feelings haven't caught up yet.
- Trust God's Justice — Believe He sees, knows, and will make things right.
- Keep Your Heart Tender — Invite God to soften any hardness toward Him or others.
- Stay Open to Relationships — Be willing to reconnect in healthy ways and avoid isolation.

See Also: Anger, Bitterness, Idolatry, Perfectionism, Pride, Rejection, Self-Hatred

COMPARISON LOOP RESET

Destructive Pattern:
Insecurity → Comparison → Jealousy or Self-Rejection → Striving or Sabotage → Resentment → Bitterness → Shame or Pride → Destruction

Often Triggered By:
Fear, Jealousy, Comparison, Self-Hatred

How This Loop May Feel in Real Life:
You feel insecure or unsure about your worth → You start comparing yourself to others' achievements, appearance, or relationships → This leads to jealousy, envy, or tearing yourself down → You either strive to "catch up" or subtly sabotage others' success → Resentment and bitterness creep in, leaving you exhausted and joyless → Over time, you feel ashamed for not measuring up or prideful when you think you do, keeping you stuck in the cycle.

Declarations (with Scripture):
- I am fearfully and wonderfully made. (Psalm 139:14)
- I rejoice with those who rejoice. (Romans 12:15)
- My calling is unique and valuable. (Ephesians 2:10)
- I fix my eyes on Jesus, not on others. (Hebrews 12:2)
- I live from gratitude, not comparison. (1 Thessalonians 5:18)

Sample Prayer:
Jesus, I repent for comparing myself to others and believing I'm not enough. I renounce envy, self-rejection, and striving. Help me celebrate others and rest in who You made me to be. I receive Your love and joyfully step into my unique calling.

Journal Prompts:
- Where has comparison stolen my joy?
- What is one unique way God has gifted me?
- How can I guard my heart against envy and choose celebration?

Steps that Interrupt the Comparison Loop:
- Secure Identity in Christ — Rest in God's love and acceptance.
- Celebrate Others — Choose joy in their success.
- Recognize Your Unique Calling — Value your God-given gifts.
- Rest in God's Timing — Trust His process for your life.
- Serve with Joy — Give freely without competition.
- Guard the Heart from Envy — Stay thankful and humble.

See Also: Anger, Bitterness, Idolatry, Perfectionism, Pride, Rejection, Self-Hatred

CONTROL LOOP RESET

Destructive Pattern:
Control → Disconnection → Rejection (Real or Perceived) → Offense → Unforgiveness → Hopelessness → Destruction

Often Triggered By:
Fear, Rejection

How This Loop May Feel in Real Life:
You face uncertainty and feel anxious → To avoid disappointment, you try to control people, circumstances, or outcomes → This makes others pull away feeling micromanaged, manipulated, or controlled → Their distance feels like rejection → Hurt turns into offense and resentment → You hold onto unforgiveness, cutting yourself and others off from grace and connection → Hope fades, leaving you weary and spiritually drained → Eventually, you want to end the relationship as a form of relief or self-protection.

Declarations (with Scripture):
- I surrender to God's good and perfect will. (Romans 12:2)
- I cast all my cares on Him because He cares for me. (1 Peter 5:7)
- I do not lean on my own understanding. (Proverbs 3:5–6)
- I stay connected to the body of Christ in humility. (Ephesians 4:2-3)
- My hope is anchored in the Lord. (Hebrews 6:19)

Sample Prayer:
God, I lay down my need to be in control. I repent for trying to force outcomes, withdraw from others, or protect myself through control. I trust Your ways, even when they don't match mine. Teach me to walk in humility, trust deeply, and live with open hands and a surrendered heart.

Journal Prompts:
- What do I feel the need to control right now?
- How has my control impacted my connection with others?
- What would completely trusting God look like in this area?

Steps that Interrupt the Control Loop:
- Surrender the Need to Control — Lay down outcomes and trust God's sovereignty.
- Choose Trust Over Fear — Believe that His ways and timing are good, even when uncertain.
- Stay Connected in Humility — Value relationships more than being "in charge."
- Release Offense Quickly — Let go of hurt before it hardens into bitterness.
- Forgive and Extend Grace — Walk in mercy instead of holding grudges.
- Live with Open Hands — Rest in God's leadership and live free from striving.

See Also: Abandonment, Anger, Bitterness, Fear, Perfectionism, Pride, Rejection, Self-Hatred

FEAR LOOP RESET

Destructive Pattern:
Fear → Anxiety → Catastrophizing → Hesitation → Withdrawal → Missed Opportunity → Blame → Condemnation → Hopelessness → Paralysis → Destruction

Often Triggered By:
An Unexpected Threat (Real or Perceived)

How This Loop May Feel in Real Life:
An unexpected threat (real or perceived) causes you to react in fear → Your body's initial response is a spike in anxiety → The anxiety triggers your mind to begin catastrophizing → Those mental tapes cause you to hesitate not wanting to make things worse → You withdraw, thinking it's towards safety → You miss opportunities because you pulled away → Eventually, you experience blame (from you or others) → The condemnation takes hold → Causing hope to dim → Leaving you paralyzed not wanting to move forward until everything is better → Which eventually leads to destruction.

Declarations (with Scripture):
- God has not given me a spirit of fear. (2 Timothy 1:7)
- I trust in the Lord with all my heart. (Proverbs 3:5-6)
- I am bold and courageous because God is with me. (Joshua 1:9)
- I release control and rest in God's peace. (Philippians 4:6–7)
- I am confident that the Lord is my helper. (Hebrews 13:6)

Sample Prayer:
Lord, I confess the fear that has gripped my heart. I repent for trying to control what only You can lead. I renounce the spirit of fear and every agreement I've made with anxiety, blame, or avoidance. Fill me with Your peace and boldness. I choose to trust You fully and walk in faith.

Journal Prompts:
- What fear do I keep returning to?
- Where am I using control instead of trust?
- What would bold faith look like in this area?

Steps that Interrupt the Fear Loop:
- Name the Fear — Identify what you're afraid of and bring it into the light.
- Surrender Control to God — Release the need to manipulate outcomes and trust God.
- Receive His Perfect Love — Let God's love drive out fear and bring peace to your heart.
- Take a Step of Faith — Choose obedience even when it feels risky or uncertain.
- Stay Connected in Truth and Community — Surround yourself with Scripture and supportive believers who remind you of God's promises.
- Walk in Courage and Hope — Choose to take a step of faith daily with God's presence and faithfulness.

See Also: Control, Numbness, Overwhelm, Rejection, Trauma

GRIEF LOOP RESET

Destructive Pattern:
Grief → Numbness → Withdrawal → Suppression → Anger → Bitterness → Hopelessness → Death Agreements → Destruction

Often Triggered By:
Loss or Potential Loss, Missed Expectations

How This Loop May Feel in Real Life:
Loss hits hard and leaves a deep ache → You shut down emotionally, feeling numb → You pull away from others to avoid vulnerability or having to explain yourself → Pain gets stuffed down instead of expressed → Unprocessed sorrow turns into anger → Anger calcifies into bitterness → Hope drains away as you see all that's wrong → You begin agreeing with hopeless lies that perpetuate your view → Life feels empty and heavy making you want to leave, give up, or escape.

Declarations (with Scripture):
- The Lord is close to the brokenhearted. (Psalm 34:18)
- I do not grieve without hope. (1 Thessalonians 4:13)
- God collects all my tears and sees my sorrow. (Psalm 56:8)
- His joy will come in the morning. (Psalm 30:5)
- He is restoring my soul. (Psalm 23:3)

Sample Prayer:
God, I bring my grief and sorrow before You. I've been trying to carry this weight alone. I repent for shutting down and withdrawing from You and others. I receive Your comfort and healing presence. Help me grieve honestly and trust You to bring beauty from ashes.

Journal Prompts:
- What have I lost that still aches?
- Have I been honest with God about my pain?
- Where is He beginning to bring life and joy again?

Steps that Interrupt the Grief Loop:
- Acknowledge the Loss — Give yourself permission to name, feel, and bring the pain to God.
- Bring Sorrow into God's Presence — Invite Him to meet you in the rawness of grief.
- Express Honestly and Safely — Share your holy lament through prayer, journaling, or with trusted people.
- Release Anger and Bitterness — Surrender resentment and let His comfort in.
- Anchor Hope in Christ — Choose to believe His promises and eternal perspective.
- Rebuild with Joy and Purpose — Allow God to turn mourning into dancing and lead you into renewed life.

See Also: Numbness, Isolation, Suppressed Anger, Trauma

IDENTITY CONFUSION LOOP RESET

Destructive Pattern:

Accusation or Lack of Affirmation → Confusion → People-Pleasing → Compromise → Regret → Shame → Self-Rejection → Despair → Destruction

Often Triggered By:

Criticism, Rejection, Lack of Affirmation

How This Loop May Feel in Real Life:

You experience criticism, rejection, or a lack of affirmation → You start doubting your worth and who you are → To keep the peace or be accepted, you begin changing parts of yourself to match what others expect → Over time, you compromise your values, feeling disconnected from your true self → The choices leave you with regret and an underlying shame → You reject yourself for "not being enough" or "being too much" → Despair sets in, making it hard to believe you'll ever truly know who you are or belong anywhere.

Declarations (with Scripture):

- I am fearfully and wonderfully made. (Psalm 139:14)
- I am a child of God and co-heir with Christ. (Romans 8:16–17)
- I live to please God, not man. (Galatians 1:10)
- I am chosen, holy, and dearly loved. (Colossians 3:12)
- My identity is hidden in Christ. (Colossians 3:3)

Sample Prayer:

Father, I renounce every lie that has confused my identity or distorted my worth. I repent for compromising truth to be accepted. I receive Your affirmation and truth. Teach me to walk boldly in who You say I am, not who others expect me to be.

Journal Prompts:

- Where have I let others define my worth or direction?
- What core truth is God speaking about who I am?
- What would confidence in my God-given identity look like?

Steps that Interrupt the Identity Confusion Loop:

- Recognize the Lie — Identify false beliefs or labels that have shaped how you see yourself and your interactions with others.
- Receive God's Truth — Root your worth and identity in Scripture and His voice.
- Stand Firm in Conviction — Live according to God's standards, even if it costs approval.
- Please God, Not People — Shift your focus from others to God's delight in you.
- Accept Yourself in Christ — Embrace your God-designed personality, gifts, and calling.
- Walk in Clarity and Confidence — Move forward as a secure son or daughter of God.

See Also: Control, Fear, Comparison, Rejection

IDOLATRY LOOP RESET

Destructive Pattern:
Discontent → Idol or Substitute Source → Temporary Relief → Attachment → Guilt → Spiritual Numbness → Hardness of Heart → Destruction

Often Triggered By:
Restlessness, Dissatisfaction, Fear, Pride

How This Loop May Feel in Real Life:
You feel restless, dissatisfied, or unfulfilled → Instead of running to God, you turn to a person, achievement, habit, or comfort to meet that need → It gives you a temporary lift, but you start to depend on it more and more → Guilt creeps in because you know your heart is divided → Over time, your passion for God fades and spiritual numbness sets in → Your heart grows hard, making it harder to hear His voice → You feel trapped, far from Him, and wonder how you drifted so far.

Declarations (with Scripture):
- I worship the Lord my God and serve Him only. (Matthew 4:10)
- I will have no other gods before Him. (Exodus 20:3)
- Jesus is my source of life and joy. (John 15:5; Psalm 16:11)
- I cast down every idol and fix my eyes on Jesus. (Hebrews 12:2; 2 Corinthians 10:5) My heart is fully His. (2 Chronicles 16:9)

Sample Prayer:
Father, I repent for placing other things above You. I renounce idolatry in all its forms—relationships, success, comfort, or control. I return to You as my first love. Cleanse me, fill me, and reestablish Yourself as the center of my life.

Journal Prompts:
- What have I been running to for comfort instead of God?
- What idols need to be torn down in my life?
- What would complete surrender look like right now?

Steps that Interrupt the Idolatry Loop:
- Acknowledge Misplaced Affections — Be honest about what's been taking God's place.
- Tear Down Idols — Remove what feeds the attachment, even if it's costly.
- Return to God — Reignite passion for God through prayer, worship, testimonies, and time sitting in His presence.
- Receive Fulfillment in Christ — Let Him meet the needs and desires of your heart.
- Establish Daily Worship — Practice consistent praise and surrender to God.
- Walk in Dependence on God — Lean on His strength and guidance in every area of life.

See Also: Addiction, Perversion, Pride, Comparison, Identity Confusion, Control

ISOLATION LOOP RESET

Destructive Pattern:
Pain or Disappointment → Withdrawal → Distrust → Self-Protection → Lack of Community → Loneliness → Despair → Destruction

Often Triggered By:
Hurt, Betrayal, Criticism, Correction, Pain

How This Loop May Feel in Real Life:
You experience hurt, betrayal, or disappointment → Instead of processing it in a healthy manner, you pull back from people → You start to distrust others and protect yourself from further pain → Over time, you avoid community, thinking you're safer alone → Loneliness creeps in and your heart feels heavy → You begin to wonder if you even belong anywhere, leaving you discouraged and disconnected.

Declarations (with Scripture):
- God sets the lonely in families. (Psalm 68:6)
- I am part of the body of Christ. (1 Corinthians 12:27)
- I do not carry my burdens alone. (Galatians 6:2)
- I walk in the light and in fellowship with others. (1 John 1:7)
- I belong and I matter. (Romans 12:5)

Sample Prayer:
Lord, I bring You my pain and disappointment. I repent for isolating, hiding, and building walls to protect myself. I renounce every lie that says I'm better off alone. Help me open up again, risk connection, and find safety in Your presence and among Your people.

Journal Prompts:
- What pain or distrust caused me to withdraw?
- Who are safe people I can reconnect with?
- What does healthy belonging look like in this season?

Steps that Interrupt the Isolation Loop:
- Name the Pain — Identify the wound that led you to withdraw.
- Bring It to God and Safe People — Share honestly with Him and a trusted community.
- Rebuild Trust — Take small steps toward openness.
- Open Your Heart Again — Allow yourself to be known without fear.
- Reconnect to Community — Commit to showing up consistently.
- Live in Mutual Care — Give and receive support in healthy relationships.

See Also: Abandonment, Betrayal, Comparison, Fear, Grief, Rejection, Trauma, Victim

NUMBNESS LOOP RESET

Destructive Pattern:
Pain or Overwhelm → Emotional Numbness → Disengagement → Passivity → Isolation → Depression → Hopelessness → Destruction

Often Triggered By:
Trauma, Stress, Loss, Disappointment

How This Loop May Feel in Real Life:
Something hits hard—trauma, ongoing stress, or deep disappointment—and instead of facing the pain, you shut down inside → Your emotions feel muted, almost like you're watching life happen from behind a glass wall → You pull back from activities, conversations, and even from God → Passivity takes over, and you move through life on autopilot → Isolation grows, and the distance from others deepens the heaviness → Depression creeps in, making hope feel far away → You start to believe nothing will change, and disconnection becomes the default.

Declarations (with Scripture):
- God restores my soul and renews my mind. (Psalm 23:3; Romans 12:2)
- I will not grow weary—He gives me strength. (Isaiah 40:29–31)
- The Lord revives my heart and my spirit. (Isaiah 57:15)
- I am connected to Christ and His body. (John 15:5; 1 Corinthians 12:27)
- I am not alone in the dark—His light surrounds me. (Psalm 139:11-12)

Sample Prayer:
Jesus, I confess that I've felt emotionally shut down and disconnected. I repent for retreating into numbness and passivity. I renounce every spirit of heaviness, avoidance, and despair. Reconnect me to Your presence and awaken my heart to feel again. Breathe fresh life into me.

Journal Prompts:
- What emotion have I been avoiding or suppressing?
- Where do I sense God inviting me back into connection?
- What does it mean to feel safely in His presence?

Steps that Interrupt the Numbness Loop:
- Acknowledge the Pain — Bring the source of pain and feelings of overwhelm into God's presence instead of burying it.
- Renounce the Lie — Break the agreement with the lie that you are better off not feeling.
- Take One Step — Choose one simple, life-giving action that breaks passivity and do it.
- Reconnect with Safe Community — Let trusted people help you carry the weight.
- Anchor Your Hope — Remember God's promises and purposes for your life again.
- Risk Feeling Again — Step out of autopilot and live present, grounded, and free.

See Also: Apathy, Fear, Grief, Isolation, Trauma

If in crisis (U.S.): call/text 988. If in immediate danger: 911

OVERWHELM LOOP RESET

Destructive Pattern:
Overwhelm → Anxiety → Control or Paralysis → Exhaustion → Despair → Hopelessness → Destruction

Often Triggered By:
Unexpected Stress, Loss, Pain, or Inadequacy

How This Loop May Feel in Real Life:
Life feels like it's piling on faster than you can handle → Deadlines, responsibilities, or crises begin to stretch you beyond capacity → Anxiety kicks in: your mind races, your body feels restless, and peace feels out of reach → You either scramble to over-control every detail or shut down in paralysis, unable to act → Both routes lead to exhaustion, emotionally and physically → As the cycle drags on, despair whispers, "Things will never get better" → Hopelessness settles in, convincing you there's no way forward → Left unchecked, the weight of overwhelm crushes your spirit and leads toward destructive choices.

Declarations (with Scripture):
- I cast all my cares on the Lord, for He cares for me. (1 Peter 5:7)
- I am not alone—God strengthens me and holds me. (Isaiah 41:10)
- I receive rest for my soul from Jesus. (Matthew 11:28–30)
- God gives me wisdom and orders my steps. (Proverbs 16:9; James 1:5)
- My hope is anchored in the faithfulness of God. (Hebrews 6:19)

Sample Prayer:
Father, I confess that I've been overwhelmed by the pressures and demands around me. I repent for trying to control everything or giving in to paralysis and despair. I release my burdens to You. Teach me to abide, to rest in Your presence, and to walk with renewed hope. Anchor me in Your peace and restore my strength.

Journal Prompts:
- What circumstances or responsibilities are causing overwhelm?
- Where have I tried to take control instead of surrendering to God?
- How can I build rhythms of rest, trust, and peace into my life?

Steps that Interrupt the Overwhelm Loop:
- Pause and Breathe — Step out of the swirl and center yourself in God's presence.
- Cast Your Cares on Him — Release the specific burdens you're carrying into His hands.
- Surrender Control — Refuse the lie that everything depends on you.
- Rest in Him — Take intentional moments of quiet, prayer, or worship to recharge.
- Seek His Wisdom — Ask God for direction and clarity for next steps.
- Take One Step at a Time — Move forward in small, faith-filled actions anchored in hope.

See Also: Apathy, Addiction, Control, Fear, Grief, Isolation, Perfectionism, Trauma

PERFECTIONISM OR PERFORMANCE LOOP RESET

Destructive Pattern:

Rejection (often through correction) → Pressure → Fear (of failure and further rejection) → Desire for Control → Lack of Trust → Overworking or Perfectionism → Exhaustion → Shame → Self-Condemnation → Burnout → Destruction

Often Triggered By:

Correction, Criticism, Rejection (or Fear of It)

How This Loop May Feel in Real Life:

You receive correction, criticism, or feel rejected → This sparks pressure to "do better" or prove your worth → Fear of failure drives you to over-control every detail → You stop trusting others (and even God) with outcomes → Overworking and perfectionism become your coping strategy → Exhaustion sets in, but you push harder to keep up → Mistakes or missed expectations trigger shame → Self-condemnation grows, making you believe you'll never be enough → Burnout leaves you empty, disconnected, and hopeless.

Declarations (with Scripture):

- I am saved by grace, not by performance. (Ephesians 2:8-9)
- I am already accepted and approved in Christ. (Romans 15:7)
- I do all things in His strength, not mine. (Philippians 4:13)
- I find rest in Jesus, not burnout. (Matthew 11:28–30)
- I live to please God, not to impress people. (Galatians 1:10)

Sample Prayer:

Lord, I confess my striving and fear of not being enough. I repent for living for approval and tying my worth to performance. I renounce perfectionism and receive the peace that comes from knowing I'm loved and accepted. Help me serve from rest and live with joy in my identity.

Journal Prompts:

- Where do I feel the need to prove myself?
- What happens when I slow down and rest?
- How can I let go of pressure and embrace grace?

Steps that Interrupt the Perfectionism or Performance Loop:

- Rest in God's Grace — Receive His acceptance apart from performance.
- Root Identity in Sonship — Remember you are loved and approved as His child.
- Release Control and Unrealistic Expectations — Trust God and others with outcomes instead of over-managing.
- Serve from Rest, Not Striving — Let joy, not pressure, fuel your work.
- Embrace Weakness with Humility — Allow God's strength to shine in your limits.
- Live Free from Comparison — Walk in purpose, grateful for your unique calling.

See Also: Control, Fear, Perversion, Pride, Rejection

PERVERSION LOOP RESET

Destructive Pattern:
Wound or Exposure → Curiosity → Indulgence → Guilt → Shame → Secrecy → Craving → Escalation → Destruction

Often Triggered By:
Abuse, A Wound, Early Exposure to Sexual Things, Fear, Overwhelm, Rejection

How This Loop May Feel in Real Life:
You experience a wound, betrayal, or early exposure to unhealthy sexual images or situations → Curiosity is stirred, leading you to explore thoughts, fantasies, or behaviors you know aren't God's best → Indulgence brings a temporary rush but quickly turns into guilt → Shame pushes you to hide instead of seeking help → Secrecy feeds the craving, making temptation feel even stronger or more exciting → What started small escalates, demanding more to feel the same effect → You feel trapped, dirty, and far from God, unsure if you can ever be free.

Declarations (with Scripture):
- I am cleansed and set apart by God. (1 Corinthians 6:11)
- I walk in purity and truth. (Psalm 119:9)
- I am not a slave to sin but a servant of righteousness. (Romans 6:18)
- I take every thought captive to obey Christ. (2 Corinthians 10:5)
- My body is a temple of the Holy Spirit. (1 Corinthians 6:19-20)

Sample Prayer:
Jesus, I bring every perversion, wound, and secret into the light. I renounce all spirits of lust, fantasy, confusion, and shame. Cleanse me and restore my purity. Help me walk in truth, protect my thoughts, and renew my mind in Your love.

Journal Prompts:
- Where did the door to perversion or false intimacy first open?
- What lies have I believed about my worth or desires?
- What does sexual wholeness look like in Christ?

Steps that Interrupt the Perversion Loop:
- Bring Wounds into the Light — Refuse secrecy. Invite God and safe people into your healing.
- Confess and Renounce — Break agreement with lust, fantasy, and shame.
- Receive Cleansing and Grace — Accept God's full forgiveness and cleansing.
- Establish Purity and Accountability — Put guardrails in place with trusted people.
- Renew the Mind with Truth — Replace lies with God's Word about your identity.
- Live from True Identity in Christ — Pursue intimacy with God, not false substitutes.

See Also: Addiction, Identity Confusion, Control, Overwhelm, Perfectionism, Shame, Trauma

PRIDE LOOP RESET

Destructive Pattern:

Pride → Independence → Refusal to Receive Help → Rejection of Others → Isolation → Frustration → Stagnation → Judgment of Others → Fall/Failure → Shame → Self-Hatred → Destruction

Often Triggered By:

Need for Approval, Fear, Rejection, Self-Reliance

How This Loop May Feel in Real Life:

You feel confident in your own ability and resist relying on others → When challenges arise, you push through alone, not wanting to appear weak → Advice or support from others feels unnecessary or even intrusive → Rejecting help pushes people away, and you convince yourself they don't understand → Isolation leaves you frustrated and stuck because everything falls on your shoulders → In that place, you grow critical, noticing faults in others while ignoring your own → Eventually a failure exposes your limits, and shame comes crashing in → The very independence you trusted now leaves you cut off from God's grace and alone with self-hatred.

Declarations (with Scripture):

- God gives grace to the humble. (James 4:6)
- I trust the Lord, not my own strength. (Proverbs 3:5–6)
- I value others above myself. (Philippians 2:3–4)
- I receive correction and grow wiser. (Proverbs 12:1)
- I humble myself under God's mighty hand. (1 Peter 5:6)

Sample Prayer:

Lord, I humble myself before You. I repent for pride, self-reliance, and rejecting the help You offer through others. I renounce independence and judgment. Teach me to depend on You, to honor others, and to walk in grace. I receive Your strength in my weakness.

Journal Prompts:

- Where have I relied on myself instead of God?
- When have I resisted correction or help?
- How can I practice humility in this season?

Steps that Interrupt the Pride Loop:

- Humble Myself Before God — Choose surrender over self-reliance.
- Depend on the Spirit — Trust His strength, not my own.
- Receive Help from Others — Allow support instead of pushing it away.
- Stay Teachable — Welcome correction and wisdom.
- Honor Others — Value people above myself.
- Walk in Grace — Live lifted by God, giving Him all glory.

See Also: Control, Fear, Isolation, Rejection, Rebellion, Self-Hatred

REBELLION LOOP RESET

Destructive Pattern:

Wounding or Control by Others → Rebellion → Independence → Justification → Deception → Isolation → Sin Patterns → Hardness of Heart → Destruction

Often Triggered By:

Wounding, Control by Others, Fear

How This Loop May Feel in Real Life:

Someone in authority wounds you, controls you, or betrays your trust → Instead of processing the pain with God, you push back and refuse their influence → This fuels an independent mindset: I don't need anyone telling me what to do → You justify pulling away, convinced you're protecting yourself → Over time, lies and deception take root, making you suspicious of correction or guidance → You isolate to stay "safe," but hidden sin patterns or opposition to "being controlled" grow stronger → Your heart hardens toward authority—both God's and people's—leaving you spiritually distant and bound.

Declarations (with Scripture):

- I submit to God and resist the enemy. (James 4:7)
- I trust God's leadership in every area of my life. (Proverbs 3:5-6)
- I walk with others in humility and honor. (1 Peter 5:5)
- I delight in obeying God. (Psalm 40:8)
- I am no longer rebellious—I am yielded and free. (Ezekiel 36:26-27)

Sample Prayer:

God, I repent for rebellion and resisting Your voice. I forgive those who misused authority and caused me to close my heart. I renounce every spirit of defiance, independence, and isolation. Fill me with humility, joy in obedience, and a heart that trusts Your leadership.

Journal Prompts:

- Who do I need to forgive for misuse of authority?
- Where have I resisted godly accountability?
- What would joyful submission to God look like today?

Steps that Interrupt the Rebellion Loop:

- Forgive Wounds from Authority — Place those who misused power into God's hands.
- Submit to God's Leadership — Yield your will to His guidance in every area.
- Choose Trust Over Suspicion — Believe God works even through imperfect people.
- Walk in Healthy Accountability — Invite trusted believers to speak into your life.
- Stay Connected in Community — Refuse isolation and build strong, godly relationships.
- Obey with Joy and Humility — Follow God's direction promptly and wholeheartedly.

See Also: Anger, Bitterness, Control, Fear, Isolation, Pride, Rejection, Victim

REJECTION LOOP RESET

Destructive Pattern:

Rejection → Insecurity → Comparison → Self-Rejection → Isolation → Bitterness → Hatred → Destruction

Often Triggered By:

Harsh Words, Absence, Distance, Being Overlooked

How This Loop May Feel in Real Life:

You experience rejection — maybe through harsh words, exclusion, or being overlooked → It stings deeply and breeds insecurity, making you question your worth → To measure yourself, you begin comparing with others, but it only reinforces the feeling that you don't measure up → Self-rejection takes root, and you quietly start believing you're unlovable or not good enough → To protect yourself, you withdraw into isolation, cutting off opportunities for genuine connection → Bitterness grows toward those who hurt you or even toward God for allowing the pain → Left unchecked, it hardens into hatred, not just toward others but even toward yourself → Eventually, rejection consumes your perspective, sabotaging relationships and leading toward destruction.

Declarations (with Scripture):

- I am fully accepted and deeply loved by God. (Ephesians 1:6; Romans 8:38-39)
- I am secure in my identity as a child of the King. (1 John 3:1; Galatians 4:7)
- I choose to celebrate others without comparison. (Romans 12:10; Galatians 5:26)
- I belong in the body of Christ. (1 Corinthians 12:27)
- I reject bitterness and receive the joy of connection. (Hebrews 12:15; Psalm 133:1)

Sample Prayer:

Father, I repent for agreeing with the lie that I am unwanted or unworthy. I renounce the spirit of rejection and every false belief that has kept me bound in comparison and isolation. I receive Your truth: I am chosen, accepted, and loved. Heal every place rejection has taken root, and fill me with Your love that overflows to others.

Journal Prompts:

- Where did I first feel rejected, and what did I believe in that moment?
- How has rejection shaped the way I relate to others?
- What does God say about my identity and value?

Steps that Interrupt the Rejection Loop:

- Receive God's Love — Let His Word remind you that you are chosen and fully accepted.
- Stand Secure in Identity — Declare your worth daily as a beloved child of God.
- Reject Comparison — Celebrate others without measuring yourself against them.
- Engage in Community — Stay connected and refuse the pull of isolation.
- Extend Forgiveness and Grace — Release those who rejected you

See Also: Abandonment, Comparison, Grief, Isolation, Perfectionism, Self-Hatred, Shame, Victim

SELF-HATRED LOOP RESET

Destructive Pattern:
Abuse, Wound, or Rejection → Offense → Fear → Negative Self-Talk → Comparison → Self-Rejection → Disgust → Shame → Despair → Self-Blame → Destructive Behaviors → Reinforced Self-Hatred → Destruction

Often Triggered By:
Abuse, Wound, Rejection, or Pride

How This Loop May Feel in Real Life:
A deep wound or betrayal is unaddressed or unprocessed → When no one take responsibility for the wound an offense develops and is nurtured → Fear of other wounds make you turn inward → Your own words become weapons against yourself → You begin to amplify your flaws compared to others → Those comparisons give reason why others have or will reject you, so you reject yourself first → Eventually this leads to disgust toward yourself → The shame and despair you've felt deepen → You blame yourself for everything and act in ways that aren't healthy and eventually reinforce the hatred → The cycle leaves you feeling beyond hope.

Declarations (with Scripture):
- I am fearfully and wonderfully made. (Psalm 139:14)
- I am God's workmanship, created for good. (Ephesians 2:10)
- God delights in me. (Zephaniah 3:17)
- I reject lies and choose the truth about who I am. (John 8:32)
- I love myself the way God loves me. (Mark 12:31)

Sample Prayer:
Father, I renounce every word of self-hatred, vow made, and the lies I've believed about my worth. I repent for cursing what You created in love. I receive Your delight in me and Your love that defines me. Heal the wounds that led to this hatred and help me live from Your truth and joy.

Journal Prompts:
- What have I said about myself that God wouldn't say?
- Where did I begin to hate or reject myself?
- What does God actually say about who I am?

Steps that Interrupt the Self-Hatred Loop:
- Receive God's Love — Let His delight define your worth.
- Renounce Lies — Break agreement with false self-beliefs and word curses.
- Embrace God's Image — Ask God to show you how he sees you.
- Speak Life Over Yourself — Replace negative self-talk with truth.
- Walk in Joyful Confidence — Stand secure in your identity as God's child.

See Also: Anger, Comparison, Grief, Isolation, Perfectionism, Rejection, Self-Hatred, Shame, Trauma, Victim

If in crisis (U.S.): call/text 988. If in immediate danger: 911

SHAME LOOP RESET

Destructive Pattern:
Shame → Fear of Rejection → Hiding → Accusation → Self-Imposed Rejection → Control or Perfectionism → Exhaustion or Breakdown → Destruction

Often Triggered By:
Mistake, Embarrassment, Insecurity, Regret, Shame

How This Loop May Feel in Real Life:
You make a mistake or remember a past failure → Fear kicks in that if people knew, they'd reject you → You hide parts of yourself, avoiding vulnerability → Accusing thoughts keep you trapped in guilt, reminding you of why you don't measure up → You start rejecting yourself before others can → You try to control how you're perceived, demanding perfection from yourself → The pressure leads to exhaustion or a breakdown → You cope in unhealthy ways, confirming the shame you felt in the first place.

Declarations (with Scripture):
- I am a new creation in Christ. (2 Corinthians 5:17)
- I am fully known and fully loved. (Romans 5:8; Psalm 139:1–4)
- There is no condemnation for me in Christ Jesus. (Romans 8:1)
- I am clothed in righteousness, not shame. (Isaiah 61:10)
- I rest in God's mercy and walk in freedom. (Hebrews 4:16)

Sample Prayer:
Jesus, thank You for carrying my shame to the cross. I renounce the lie that I am unworthy or unfixable. I repent for hiding, striving, and judging myself harshly. I receive Your grace and mercy. Teach me to live in the truth that I am deeply loved and entirely accepted by You.

Journal Prompts:
- What lie did shame teach me about myself?
- Where have I been hiding from God or others?
- How does Jesus want to restore my worth?

Steps that Interrupt the Shame Loop:
- Bring Shame to the Lord — Confess hidden things to God and safe people instead of hiding.
- Receive God's Forgiveness and Acceptance — Let His truth replace accusing lies.
- Renounce Self-Rejection — Receive God's love and agree with who God says you are.
- Embrace Grace over Perfection — Stop striving and rest in God's finished work.
- Practice Vulnerability in Safe Community — Allow others to see the real you.
- Walk in Freedom and Joy — Live out of acceptance and God's truth.

See Also: Addiction, Anger, Comparison, Isolation, Perfectionism, Rejection, Self-Hatred, Trauma, Victim

SUPPRESSED ANGER LOOP RESET

Destructive Pattern:
Anger → Silence/Suppression → Resentment → Guilt → Shame → Self-Accusation → Depression → Physical Symptoms (sickness, fatigue) → Breakdown → Destruction

Often Triggered By:
Layered Grief or Disrespect, Deep Pain

How This Loop May Feel in Real Life:
Something happens that stirs deep anger, but instead of expressing it healthily, you swallow it down → You tell yourself it's not worth the fight, but the emotion lingers under the surface → Over time, that hidden anger hardens into resentment toward a person, situation, or even God → You start feeling guilty for even being angry, which quickly slides into shame → You turn the blame inward, accusing yourself for being "too much" or "not enough" → The unprocessed weight begins to sap your energy, feeding depression and even showing up physically in your body as tension, fatigue, or illness → Eventually, the built-up pressure causes an emotional breakdown or explosive outburst, leaving you feeling even more disconnected and heavy.

Declarations (with Scripture):
- I am slow to anger and rich in love. (James 1:19–20; Psalm 145:8)
- I bring my anger to God and do not sin. (Ephesians 4:26)
- I choose forgiveness over resentment. (Mark 11:25)
- God's grace lifts guilt and shame. (Romans 8:1)
- I cast my burdens on the Lord. (Psalm 55:22)

Sample Prayer:
God, I bring my anger before You. I repent for hiding my pain and letting it fester in resentment. I renounce every spirit tied to guilt, shame, or emotional breakdown. Teach me to express my emotions truthfully, forgive fully, and live with integrity and peace.

Journal Prompts:
- What am I angry about that I've been afraid to express?
- How has suppression affected my mental and emotional health?
- What is one thing I need to say to God or others honestly?

Steps that Interrupt the Suppressed Anger Loop:
- Acknowledge the Anger — Name it honestly before God without shame.
- Process with God or a Safe Person — Let the emotion be expressed in a healthy manner.
- Identify the Root — Pinpoint the wound, unmet need, or injustice fueling the anger.
- Forgive with Courage — Release the offense, even if you must do it daily.
- Release the Burden — Give the weight to God through prayer and surrender.
- Walk in Emotional Integrity — Commit to honest, respectful expression.

See Also: Anger, Bitterness, Comparison, Grief, Isolation, Perfectionism, Rejection, Self-Hatred

TRAUMA LOOP RESET

Destructive Pattern:

Trauma → Fear → Hyper-vigilance → Isolation → Emotional Numbness → Disconnection → Despair → Destruction

Often Triggered By:

Sudden Pain or Fear, Abuse, Overwhelm, Rejection

How This Loop May Feel in Real Life:

Something painful, sudden, or deeply wounding happens → You begin to live in constant alertness, always scanning for danger → Something or someone feels unsafe, so you withdraw from others not wanting to feel that again → Emotions start to go flat, and you feel disconnected from your own heart and from people → Over time, relationships fade and loneliness grows → Hope feels distant, and despair whispers that life will never be safe or whole again → The unprocessed pain shapes how you think, feel, and live, keeping you stuck in survival mode instead of moving toward healing.

Declarations (with Scripture):

- God is near to the brokenhearted. (Psalm 34:18)
- He restores my soul. (Psalm 23:3)
- I will not fear, for He is with me. (Isaiah 41:10)
- I am being made whole in Christ. (1 Thessalonians 5:23–24)
- He turns my mourning into joy. (Jeremiah 31:13)

Sample Prayer:

God, I bring the trauma and pain I've buried. I repent for isolating, shutting down, and trying to survive without You. I renounce fear and every spirit connected to trauma. Heal my soul and restore my strength. I trust You to walk me into peace and wholeness.

Journal Prompts:

- What trauma is still shaping how I live today?
- Where has numbness taken root?
- What would healing and wholeness look like?

Steps that Interrupt the Trauma Loop

- Name the Trauma Honestly — Acknowledge what happened instead of burying it.
- Invite God into the Wound — Give the pain to God. Ask Him to drain the hurt from your life.
- Break Agreement with Fear — Refuse to let hyper-vigilance define your safety.
- Reconnect with Safe People — Choose trusted relationships that model love and stability.
- Process Emotions with Truth — Guided by God's Word, allow yourself to feel again.
- Walk in Hope and Wholeness — Embrace healing as a journey, not just survival.

See Also: Fear, Grief, Isolation, Numbness, Rejection, Self-Hatred, Shame, Trauma, Victim

If in crisis (U.S.): call/text 988. If in immediate danger: 911

VICTIM LOOP RESET

Destructive Pattern:

Injustice → Pain → Defensiveness → Offense → Justification → Blame → Powerlessness → Entitlement → Pride → Destruction

Often Triggered By:

Sin, Unfair Situations, Injustice, Betrayal

How This Loop May Feel in Real Life:

You experience an unfair situation or betrayal → The pain feels raw and personal → You become guarded and defensive, quick to protect yourself → Bitterness grows into offense, and you replay the wrong over and over → Your responses and retaliation feels justified because "they hurt me first" → Blame replaces responsibility, shifting focus to other all while keeping you stuck → You feel powerless, waiting for others to change → This turns into entitlement—believing others owe you → Pride rises, cutting you off from grace and growth → Relationships fracture, and hope fades.

Declarations (with Scripture):

- In all these things, I am more than a conqueror. (Romans 8:37)
- God is my defender and judge. (Isaiah 33:22)
- I choose to forgive and walk free. (Luke 6:37)
- I am responsible for my choices and healing. (Galatians 6:5)
- God gives me the strength to overcome. (Philippians 4:13)

Sample Prayer:

God, I bring every wound and injustice to You. I repent for blaming, justifying my sin, or staying in powerlessness. I renounce the spirit of victimhood. I choose to forgive, take ownership of my healing, and walk in the strength You give. Help me respond to life with Your authority.

Journal Prompts:

- Where have I felt powerless or mistreated?
- Have I used that pain to justify wrong behavior?
- How can I take healthy ownership today?

Steps that Interrupt the Victim Loop:

- Bring Injustice to God — Lay the wrongs before Him as your righteous Judge.
- Choose Forgiveness — Release the offender and refuse to stay bound.
- Take Responsibility — Own your healing and choices moving forward.
- Reject Powerlessness — Declare that you are more than a conqueror in Christ.
- Embrace Empowerment — Walk in the Spirit's strength, not in blame.
- Live in Humility and Freedom — Respond with grace, not pride or justifying responses.

See Also: Bitterness, Fear, Perfectionism, Pride, Rebellion, Rejection, Self-Hatred, Shame, Trauma

Part 3: Breaking Free

Worksheets and Exercises to Walk You and Others to Freedom

If you've made it this far, you've likely identified at least one loop that's been running in your life. You may have seen two or three that feed into each other. That's great news! Because then you can begin the holy work of dismantling it.

In this section, you'll learn the 6-step Freedom Framework. It's a Spirit-led process that takes you from recognizing the snare to walking free from it. This isn't theory. It's the path countless others have walked and are walking to a lasting breakthrough.

You'll move from fruit to root. From surface behaviors to buried agreements. From managing symptoms to destroying strongholds. This is where the real work happens. And you won't do it alone—the Holy Spirit is your guide.

Let's go deeper. Let's go to the root. Let's get free.

THE FREEDOM FRAMEWORK: GOING FROM THE FRUIT TO THE ROOT

We were never meant to live weighed down by hidden hurts, destructive patterns, or spiritual strongholds. Yet, many of us find ourselves caught in subtle, repeating patterns of thought, feeling, and behavior that steal or destroy our freedom and future. These worksheets are designed to be a weapon to expose those patterns and partner with the Holy Spirit to find lasting freedom, healing, and peace.

"Let us throw off everything that hinders and the sin that so easily entangles. And let us run with perseverance the race marked out for us, fixing our eyes on Jesus..." — Hebrews 12:1-2

Instructions: Just as fruit doesn't grow without a root, every fear, reaction, and struggle in your life is connected to a deeper story. The enemy uses these hidden wounds to plant lies that, if left unmanaged, create beliefs and patterns of destructive behavior. We call these cycles a destructive loop, pattern, or snare that keeps you bound.

But there is good news. You are not powerless. The Holy Spirit is inviting you to go from only seeing the visible 'fruit' of your life to identifying the planted lies and beliefs that took 'root' in the wounds of your soul. For each step, there are companion worksheets to help you. Take your time, return as often as needed. Remember, you were created for freedom. Don't settle for less.

STEP 1. FIND THE SNARE(S)
Psalm 139:23-24; Romans 7:19

Check the boxes or indicate below what keeps tripping you up? What issue keeps surfacing over and over again in your life? This is the fruit, not the root, so just name it without judgment. You may feel stuck, you may blow up at your kids, or you may keep returning to an addictive behavior. Just name it.

❏ Abandonment	❏ Control	❏ Gaming	❏ Picking/ticks	❏ Smoking / Chew
❏ Abortion	❏ Corruption	❏ Gossip	❏ Pornography	❏ Strife
❏ Abuse	❏ Cutting	❏ Greed	❏ Prescript. drugs	❏ Sugar
❏ Accusation	❏ Denial	❏ Hatred	❏ Pride	❏ Technology
❏ Addictions	❏ Depression	❏ Insecure	❏ Rage	❏ Theft
❏ Adultery	❏ Despair	❏ Isolation	❏ Rebellion	❏ Thoughts of Suicide
❏ Alcohol	❏ Divisions	❏ Jealousy	❏ Rejection	❏ Unbelief
❏ Anger	❏ Divorce	❏ Legalism	❏ Revenge	❏ Unforgiveness
❏ Anorexia	❏ Doubt	❏ Love of money	❏ Secrecy	❏ Vandalism
❏ Anxiety	❏ Drugs _____	❏ Low self-esteem	❏ Self-Harm	❏ Violence
❏ Apathy	❏ Envy	❏ Lying	❏ Self-Hatred	❏ War
❏ Bitterness	❏ Escape	❏ Manipulation	❏ Sex	❏ Withdrawal
❏ Bribery	❏ Family Splits	❏ Masturbation	❏ Sexual Immorality	❏ Workaholism
❏ Bulimia	❏ Fear	❏ Neglect	❏ Shame	❏ Worthlessness
❏ Comparison	❏ Food	❏ Nightmares	❏ Silent Treatment	
❏ Competition	❏ Fraud	❏ Panic Attacks	❏ Slander	
❏ Compulsive ____	❏ Frustration	❏ Passivity	❏ Sleep	
❏ Condemnation	❏ Gambling	❏ Perfectionism	❏ Sleep aids	

STEP 2. TRACE THE DESTRUCTIVE LOOP
James 1:14-15; Proverbs 26:11

Go back to the most recent time this snare showed up. What led up to it? What resulted from it? What did you feel right before it happened? What decisions did you make in response to those feelings? How did those decisions make you feel afterward? Trace the entire sequence of events and feelings that led you deeper into the cycle. Feel free to use the following companion sheets to trace the loop.

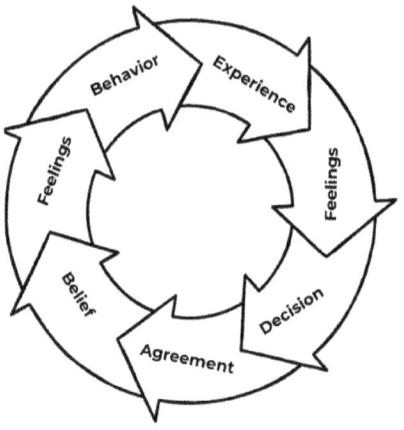

Go back to the most recent time this snare showed up. What led up to that moment?
_____
_____

What triggered the situation? Put another way, what typically starts this cycle?
_____
_____

Initial Feeling: That event or experience caused you to feel what? What emotion hit first?
_____
_____

How do you typically react when you feel that? What decision(s) did you make because of those feelings?
_____
_____

That decision likely reinforced or formed a belief. What was it? For instance, was there a lie that all of this 'proved' to be true? What did you begin to believe about God, yourself, or others?
_____
_____
_____

That belief reinforced other feelings and behaviors. How did you feel or act next?:
_____
_____

Common Emotions

Emotions can help you identify the aspects of your life that point to the root issues. Use this list as a primer to determine what you're feeling.

❏ ANGER	❏ SAD	❏ FEARFUL	❏ DISGUSTED	❏ HAPPY	❏ SURPRISED
❏ Aggressive	❏ Abandoned	❏ Alienated	❏ Appalled	❏ Accepted	❏ Amazed
❏ Annoyed	❏ Ache	❏ Anxious	❏ Avoiding	❏ Amused	❏ Astonished
❏ Ballistic	❏ Ashamed	❏ Creepy	❏ Awful	❏ Aroused	❏ Awe
❏ Bitter	❏ Blue	❏ Disturbed	❏ Detestable	❏ Calm	❏ Bewildered
❏ Catatonic	❏ Depressed	❏ Dread	❏ Disapproving	❏ Cheeky	❏ Confused
❏ Critical	❏ Desolate	❏ Excluded	❏ Embarrassed	❏ Confident	❏ Creative
❏ Demanding	❏ Despair	❏ Exposed	❏ Furious	❏ Content	❏ Curious
❏ Dismissive	❏ Devastated	❏ Faint	❏ Grossed Out	❏ Correct	❏ Dazed
❏ Dissatisfaction	❏ Disappointed	❏ Frail	❏ Hesitant	❏ Courageous	❏ Disillusioned
❏ Distant	❏ Don't Care	❏ Frightened	❏ Horrified	❏ Established	❏ Dismayed
❏ Exasperated	❏ Empty	❏ Helpless	❏ Judgmental	❏ Free	❏ Distracted
❏ Frustrated	❏ Endangered	❏ Inadequate	❏ Loathing	❏ Fulfilled	❏ Dumbfounded
❏ Guarded	❏ Forgotten	❏ Inferior	❏ Nauseated	❏ Genuine	❏ Eager
❏ Harassed	❏ Fragile	❏ Insecure	❏ Outraged	❏ Hopeful	❏ Energetic
❏ Hateful	❏ Gloomy	❏ Insignificant	❏ Repelled	❏ Important	❏ Enthusiastic
❏ Heated	❏ Grief	❏ Intimidated	❏ Revolted	❏ Influential	❏ Excited
❏ Hostile	❏ Guilty	❏ Nervous	❏ Uncomfortable	❏ Interested	❏ Inspired
❏ Humiliated	❏ Heartbroken	❏ Overwhelmed		❏ Intimate	❏ Inquisitive
❏ Indignant	❏ Hurt	❏ Panicked		❏ Joyful	❏ Marveled
❏ Infuriated	❏ Inferior	❏ Persecuted		❏ Lively	❏ Passionate
❏ Insulated	❏ Isolated	❏ Rejected		❏ Loving	❏ Perplexed
❏ Jaded	❏ Left	❏ Scared		❏ Open	❏ Pumped
❏ Jealous	❏ Lonely	❏ Terrified		❏ Optimistic	❏ Puzzled
❏ Let Down	❏ Misery	❏ Threatened		❏ Peaceful	❏ Ready
❏ Mad	❏ Mournful	❏ Uneasy		❏ Playful	❏ Shocked
❏ Malicious	❏ Powerless	❏ Vulnerable	❏ BAD	❏ Powerful	❏ Shook
❏ Not Heard	❏ Remorseful	❏ Weak	❏ Apathetic	❏ Proud	❏ Speechless
❏ Numb	❏ Restrained	❏ Worried	❏ Bored	❏ Purposeful	❏ Startled
❏ Offended	❏ Sunken	❏ Worthless	❏ Busy	❏ Quiet	❏ Stunned
❏ Provoked	❏ Susceptible		❏ Exhausted	❏ Reflective	❏ Thrilled
❏ Rage	❏ Tired		❏ Indifferent	❏ Relaxed	❏ Thrown
❏ Resentful	❏ Tortured		❏ Out of Control	❏ Respected	❏ Upbeat
❏ Reserved	❏ Unfulfilled		❏ Preoccupied	❏ Rosy	❏ Valued
❏ Ridiculed	❏ Uptight		❏ Pressured	❏ Saucy	
❏ Salty	❏ Victimized		❏ Rushed	❏ Sensitive	
❏ Scorned	❏ Vulnerable		❏ Sleepy	❏ Significant	
❏ Skeptical	❏ Withdrawn		❏ Stressed	❏ Successful	
❏ Slighted			❏ Swamped	❏ Superior	
❏ Sore			❏ Tired	❏ Supported	
❏ Unattached			❏ Unfocused	❏ Sure	
❏ Unseen			❏ Uninterested	❏ Thankful	
❏ Violated			❏ Weary	❏ Trusting	

Common Behaviors, Responses, & Sin Patterns

Use this list as a primer to identify ways you respond or behave. These behaviors and responses can help point to the root. Note, they probably aren't the root. They are more likely to be other fruits.

- ❏ Abandonment
- ❏ Abortion
- ❏ Abuse
- ❏ Accusation
- ❏ Addictions
- ❏ Adultery
- ❏ Alcohol
- ❏ Anger
- ❏ Anorexia
- ❏ Anxiety
- ❏ Apathy
- ❏ Bitterness
- ❏ Bribery
- ❏ Bulimia
- ❏ Comparison
- ❏ Competition
- ❏ Compulsive ____
- ❏ Condemnation
- ❏ Control
- ❏ Corruption
- ❏ Cutting
- ❏ Denial
- ❏ Depression
- ❏ Despair
- ❏ Divisions
- ❏ Divorce
- ❏ Doubt
- ❏ Drugs ____
- ❏ Envy
- ❏ Escape
- ❏ Family Splits
- ❏ Fear
- ❏ Food
- ❏ Fraud
- ❏ Frustration
- ❏ Gambling
- ❏ Gaming
- ❏ Gossip
- ❏ Greed
- ❏ Hatred
- ❏ Insecure
- ❏ Isolation
- ❏ Jealousy
- ❏ Legalism
- ❏ Love of money
- ❏ Low self-esteem
- ❏ Lying
- ❏ Manipulation
- ❏ Masturbation
- ❏ Neglect
- ❏ Nightmares
- ❏ Panic Attacks
- ❏ Passivity
- ❏ Perfectionism
- ❏ Picking/ticks
- ❏ Pornography
- ❏ Prescript. drugs
- ❏ Pride
- ❏ Rage
- ❏ Rebellion
- ❏ Rejection
- ❏ Revenge
- ❏ Secrecy
- ❏ Self-Harm
- ❏ Self-Hatred
- ❏ Sex
- ❏ Sexual Immorality
- ❏ Shame
- ❏ Silent Treatment
- ❏ Slander
- ❏ Sleep
- ❏ Sleep aids
- ❏ Smoking / Chew
- ❏ Strife
- ❏ Sugar
- ❏ Technology
- ❏ Theft
- ❏ Thoughts of Suicide
- ❏ Unbelief
- ❏ Unforgiveness
- ❏ Vandalism
- ❏ Violence
- ❏ War
- ❏ Withdrawal
- ❏ Workaholism
- ❏ Worthlessness

Common Lies & Beliefs (Roots)

Use this list as a primer to identify roots that have caused negative fruit in your life. These behaviors and responses can help point to the root.

1. LIES OF ISOLATION & PRIDE
- ❏ I ask too much of myself or others.
- ❏ I can't trust others to help.
- ❏ I must do it on my own.
- ❏ I'm an inconvenience.
- ❏ I can do it myself.
- ❏ I'll always _____.
- ❏ I'll never _____.
- ❏ I hate _____.

2. LIES OF SPIRITUAL CONDEMNATION
- ❏ I'm on shaky spiritual ground.
- ❏ My salvation is in question.
- ❏ I must compete for God's love.
- ❏ I'm unworthy.
- ❏ I've gone too far.
- ❏ I can't hear God's voice.
- ❏ I can't trust God.
- ❏ The church can't be trusted.

3. LIES OF INADEQUACY OR FAILURE
- ❏ I'd be better off if I were _____.
- ❏ I'm not enough.
- ❏ I'll never measure up.
- ❏ I'm not good enough.
- ❏ I'm inadequate.
- ❏ I'm insignificant.
- ❏ I'm broken.
- ❏ I'm hopeless.
- ❏ I'm worthless.
- ❏ My voice doesn't matter.

4. LIES OF REJECTION & ABANDONMENT
- ❏ I'm unwanted.
- ❏ I don't belong.
- ❏ People will always leave.
- ❏ I'm not wanted.
- ❏ I'm unloved.
- ❏ I'm the black sheep.
- ❏ I'm unable to fit in.
- ❏ I'm an inconvenience.
- ❏ I'm unprotected.
- ❏ I must compete for God's love.

5. LIES INVOLVING YOUR WORLD VIEW
- ❏ There is no hope for _____.
- ❏ Everyone _____.
- ❏ People will always leave me.
- ❏ I can't trust anyone.
- ❏ People only love me for what I do.
- ❏ If they really knew me, they'd reject me.
- ❏ People are dangerous.
- ❏ No one understands me.
- ❏ _____ always happens to me.
- ❏ If something is good, it will be taken away.
- ❏ Things will never change.

6. LIES ABOUT WHO GOD IS
- ❏ God can't or won't _____.
- ❏ God doesn't want to help me.
- ❏ God doesn't have good gifts for me.
- ❏ God has forgotten me.
- ❏ God has left me.
- ❏ God hasn't or won't forgive me.
- ❏ God has turned His back on me.
- ❏ God is distant.
- ❏ God's love has limits.
- ❏ God will take good things from me.
- ❏ God blesses others, but will never bless me.

"We demolish arguments and every pretension that sets itself up against the knowledge of God, and we take captive every thought to make it obedient to Christ." — 2 Cor 10:4-5 (NIV)

Recognizing the pattern is the first step toward freedom. Now, we're going to use God's Word as a weapon to name the snare and expose its hidden root. We have divine power to demolish strongholds and to take every thought captive, making it obedient to Christ.

STEP 3. CALL IT OUT
Ephesians 5:11; James 5:16

Now that you've traced the pattern, let's call it out by name. Look through the list of destructive loops below and identify the one that sounds most familiar. Naming it is a key strategic move in the spiritual battle.

- ❏ Abandonment
- ❏ Betrayal
- ❏ Grief
- ❏ Overwhelm
- ❏ Rejection
- ❏ Victim
- ❏ Accusation
- ❏ Bitterness
- ❏ Identity Confusion
- ❏ Perfectionism
- ❏ Self-Hatred
- ❏ Addiction
- ❏ Comparison
- ❏ Idolatry
- ❏ Perversion
- ❏ Shame
- ❏ Anger
- ❏ Control
- ❏ Isolation
- ❏ Pride
- ❏ Suppressed Anger
- ❏ Apathy
- ❏ Fear
- ❏ Numbness
- ❏ Rebellion
- ❏ Trauma

STEP 4. SEE IT EVERYWHERE
Matthew 7:16; Luke 6:45

The enemy often uses the same tactic in different areas of our lives. Now that you've named the loop, where else have you seen this pattern show up in a similar way? Consider relationships, work, finances, health, parenting, and ministry. Write it/them down below.

_____
_____
_____
_____
_____
_____
_____
_____

STEP 5. DIG TO THE ROOT
Hebrews 12:15; Matthew 15:13

Remember, the 'snare' is the visible fruit or issue in your life. It developed and took 'root' because something happened. The Holy Spirit wants to expose the original wound, lie, belief, or spiritual agreement where the seed was planted, and the destructive pattern developed or was reinforced. Ask the Holy Spirit to show you the memory or moment when it all started. Mark the answer below.

MOMENTS OF TRAUMA OR CRISIS
- ❏ Near-death experience
- ❏ Car accident or natural disaster
- ❏ Medical emergencies or chronic illness
- ❏ Sudden loss of a loved one
- ❏ Being in foster care
- ❏ Watching a parent or loved one suffer
- ❏ Being caught in war, violence, or crime
- ❏ Getting lost or left behind (esp. as a child)
- ❏ Experiencing/witnessing suicide or overdose
- ❏ Witnessing domestic violence

ABUSE AND VIOLATION
- ❏ Sexual abuse or molestation
- ❏ Physical abuse or beatings
- ❏ Verbal or emotional abuse
- ❏ Being touched inappropriately
- ❏ Manipulation or gaslighting
- ❏ Coercion or spiritual abuse
- ❏ Being objectified or used

FALSE RELIGIOUS EXPERIENCES
- ❏ Fear-based preaching (God is angry, harsh, always disappointed)
- ❏ Performance-based Christianity
- ❏ Hyper-legalism or hyper-grace without truth
- ❏ Being told your emotions = lack of faith
- ❏ Misuse of prophecy or spiritual gifts
- ❏ Experiencing church betrayal or spiritual leaders falling

BULLYING AND REJECTION
- ❏ Teased about your looks, size, intelligence, etc.
- ❏ Ostracized by peers
- ❏ Racism, sexism
- ❏ Not being invited to parties
- ❏ Being chosen last or not chosen at all
- ❏ Cyberbullying or social media shaming

RELATIONAL WOUNDS
- ❏ Being abandoned by a parent
- ❏ Parents divorcing
- ❏ Emotional neglect
- ❏ Sibling rivalry or favoritism
- ❏ Being rejected or excluded
- ❏ Constant criticism from authority figures
- ❏ Lack of affection or words of affirmation
- ❏ Being compared to others (especially negatively)
- ❏ Living with an emotionally unavailable parent

SHAME-FORMING MOMENTS
- ❏ Public embarrassment or humiliation
- ❏ Being exposed for some secret
- ❏ Failing in something significant (sports, grades, calling, ministry)
- ❏ Sexual sin or premature sexual experiences
- ❏ Being told "you're too much" or "not enough"

SPIRITUAL CONFUSION OR PAIN
- ❏ Feeling like God didn't answer a prayer
- ❏ Losing someone after fervent prayer
- ❏ Not hearing God's voice when you desperately needed direction
- ❏ Feeling like you failed God
- ❏ Long "dry seasons" that led to disillusionment
- ❏ Seeing hypocrisy in leaders or the church

EMOTIONAL WITHHOLDING
- ❏ Parents never said "I love you"
- ❏ Being told to "stop crying" or "man up"
- ❏ Growing up in a home that wasn't safe
- ❏ Not being comforted in grief
- ❏ Not having a safe place to process fear, sadness, or anger

Did you make any internal vows or decisions in response? Examples: "I'll never let anyone hurt me again," "I'll never be vulnerable," "I have to be perfect," "I can't trust anyone."
_____
_____
_____
_____
_____
_____

Root Summary:
The original wound/experience: _____
The core lie that took root: _____
The agreement (vow) I made: _____

How did that wound, lie, and vow shape your relationship with others?
_____
_____
_____
_____
_____
_____

How did that wound, lie, and vow shape your identity?
_____
_____
_____
_____
_____
_____

How did that wound, lie, and vow shape your connection with God?
_____
_____
_____
_____
_____
_____

STEP 6: STEPPING INTO FREEDOM

Freedom comes not just by breaking old patterns but by actively choosing new, life-giving ones. This is about replacing the old way of doing life with a new, Spirit-led response.

The Forgiveness I Am Choosing

Forgiveness is a powerful weapon that releases you from the prison of unforgiveness. Who do you need to forgive for their role in this pain or loop? Write their names below. Then, take a moment to invite God to minister to you as you release it all to Him.

_____
_____
_____
_____
_____

Renounce, Repent, and Receive

Jesus carried our shame to the cross. Now, you have the authority to break agreements with the lies and patterns that have held you captive. Confess any agreements you've made with these patterns, renounce them, and receive God's truth and healing in their place.

What lies has the enemy whispered that you no longer want to agree with?

_____
_____
_____
_____

What truth from God's Word breaks the power of this loop and declares your identity? We recommend using the companion sheet on page 66 (the next page) to highlight declarations connected to your identity in Christ.

_____
_____
_____
_____

My New Step of Obedience

Ask the Holy Spirit, *'What is one way of responding that leads to life rather than death?'* What is one simple, life-giving action you will take this week to interrupt this loop and start a new pattern?

_____
_____
_____

Replace the Root (Lies)
A Companion Worksheet

When lies are exposed, they must be replaced with truth. Below are truth-based declarations paired with scripture to help you replace agreements and walk in renewed identity, faith, and freedom.

Declarations Related To Your Identity

I AM...
- [ ] I am forgiven and washed clean - 1 Jn 1:9
- [ ] I am righteous in Christ, not by works - 2 Cor 5:21
- [ ] I am chosen and set apart - 1 Pet 2:9
- [ ] I am free from condemnation. - Rom 8:1
- [ ] I am forgiven - Eph 1:7
- [ ] I am fearfully and wonderfully made - Ps 139:14
- [ ] I am a new creation - 2 Cor 5:17
- [ ] I am God's workmanship - Eph 2:10
- [ ] I am created for good works - Eph 2:10
- [ ] I am God's beloved child - Rom 8:15–17
- [ ] I am God's image bearer - Gen 1:27
- [ ] I am God's ambassador - 2 Cor 5:20

I CAN...
- [ ] I can do all things through Christ - Ph 4:13
- [ ] I can resist the devil, and he will flee - Ja 4:7
- [ ] I can overcome evil with good - Rom 12:21
- [ ] I can approach God with confidence - Heb 4:16
- [ ] I can love because He first loved me - 1 Jn 4:19
- [ ] I can walk in freedom - Gal 5:1
- [ ] I can speak life and truth - Pro 18:21

GOD WILL...
- [ ] God will finish what He started in me - Phil 1:6
- [ ] God will supply all I need - Phil 4:19
- [ ] God will work all things for my good - Rom 8:28
- [ ] God will never leave me - Heb 13:5
- [ ] God will lift me up in due time - 1 Pet 5:6
- [ ] God will uphold me - Is 41:10

GOD IS...
- [ ] God is my refuge and strength. - Ps 46:1
- [ ] God is faithful. - 2 Thess 3:3
- [ ] God is near to the brokenhearted - Ps 34:18
- [ ] God is for me, not against me - Rom 8:31
- [ ] God is slow to anger and rich in love - Ps 145:8
- [ ] God is my shepherd - Ps 23:1
- [ ] God is just - Heb 6:10

I HAVE...
- [ ] I have a living hope - 1 Pet 1:3
- [ ] I have peace with God through Christ - Rom 5:1
- [ ] I have the mind of Christ - 1 Cor 2:16
- [ ] I have access to the Father by the Spirit - Eph 2:18
- [ ] I have been forgiven - Col 2:13
- [ ] I have been set free - Rom 6:18
- [ ] I have been adopted - Rom 8:15
- [ ] I have been transferred out of Darkness - Col 1:13
- [ ] I have been crucified with Christ - Gal 2:20
- [ ] I have the Holy Spirit living in me - 1 Cor 3:16
- [ ] I have every spiritual blessing - Eph 1:3
- [ ] I have been redeemed by the blood - Eph 1:7
- [ ] I have been sealed with the Holy Spirit - Ep 1:13-14

I CANNOT...
- [ ] I cannot earn my salvation - Eph 2:8-9
- [ ] I cannot outrun God's mercy - Ps 23:6
- [ ] I cannot be forgotten by God - Isa 49:15-16
- [ ] I cannot be snatched out of God's hand - Jn 10:28
- [ ] I cannot be condemned if I am in Christ - Ro 8:1
- [ ] I cannot be separated from God's love - Ro 8:38–39

GOD HAS...
- [ ] God has demonstrated His love for me - Rom 5:8
- [ ] God has blessed me - Eph 1:3
- [ ] God has forgiven all my sins - Col 2:13
- [ ] God has rescued me from darkness. - Col 1:13
- [ ] God has raised me with Christ - Col 3:1
- [ ] God has made me His own - Isa 43:1

GOD IS NOT...
- [ ] God is not disappointed in me - Zeph 3:17
- [ ] God is not slow to keep His promise. - 2 Pet 3:9
- [ ] God is not withholding good from me. - Ps 84:11
- [ ] God is not absent in my pain. - Ps 34:18
- [ ] God is not distant - Psalm 145:18
- [ ] God is not counting my sins against me. - 2 Co 5:19

Morning Check-in
A Companion Worksheet

Date: _____ Day #: _____ of 90 Scripture Read: _____

EMOTIONAL AWARENESS
When I woke up how did I feel:

_____
_____
_____
_____

Hope level: _____; Peace level: _____; Confidence in God's love: _____;
    (1= none; 10=ton of it)   (1= none; 10=ton of it)   (1= none; 10=ton of it)

MORNING DECLARATION EXAMPLE

- I am forgiven and washed clean
- I am a new creation in Christ
- I am fearfully and wonderfully made
- I am chosen and dearly loved
- I am more than a conqueror
- I am a blessing, not an inconvenience

For other examples and declarations, including audio to listen to, visit: www.thedefiningplace.com/declarations-of-overcomers

PRAYER FOR TODAY

_____
_____
_____
_____
_____
_____

5 THINGS I AM GRATEFUL FOR THIS MORNING

_____
_____
_____
_____
_____

Evening Check-in
A Companion Worksheet

EVENING DECLARATION EXAMPLE

- As a child of God, I am not defined by what I do, but rather by what Christ has done for me.
- I was made in the image of God and am being transformed into the likeness of Christ.
- I am deeply loved, seen, and heard. God's thoughts about me outnumber the sand on the seashore.
- I am fearfully and wonderfully made. I am hidden in Christ and seated in heavenly places.

Emotion that was strongest today: _____

When was it the strongest and why _____
_____
_____
_____

What it revealed about my heart: _____
_____
_____
_____
_____

Did I walk in an old loop or a new Spirit-led response? (Circle one)
Old Loop | Mixed | New Response

Truth from God's Word I needed today:
_____
_____
_____
_____

How did or didn't I live as a deeply loved person today?
_____
_____
_____
_____

DAILY VICTORIES TO CELEBRATE
- ❏ Spoke identity declarations aloud
- ❏ Prayed and journaled
- ❏ Read/meditated on Scripture
- ❏ Practiced gratitude
- ❏ Chose a new response over an old pattern
- ❏ Reached out for help when needed
- ❏ Served someone else

30 Day Tracker
A Companion Worksheet

Life Impact Assessment

Rate the intensity you feel for each emotion: 1 = not at all, 10 = extremely.

Emotion	Before Beginning	Week 1	Week 2	Week 3	Week 4
Shame About My Past					
Anger Toward Those Who Hurt Me					
Fear Of Being Vulnerable					
Hopeless About Change					
Confusion About My Identity					

Life Impact Assessment

Rate improvement from 1-10 (1=much worse, 5=no change, 10=dramatically better)

Emotion	Before Beginning	Week 1	Week 2	Week 3	Week 4
Emotional Stability					
Conflict Resolution					
Decision-making					
Work Performance					
Physical Health					
Spiritual Health					

Part 4: Resources for Leaders
How to Walk Someone Through "Escaping the Enemy's Snares"

If you're a pastor, small group leader, counselor, or ministry leader, this final section is for you. You've just walked through a process designed to bring personal freedom. But Kingdom work is never just about you. We are to carry the Kingdom and love of God wherever we go.

Jesus didn't just set people free; He equipped them to do the same for others.

In the pages ahead, you'll find:

- A Quick Sheet of the steps to freedom on one side and the loops on the other.
- A leader's guide for walking others through this material
- Case studies showing how to address multiple loops at once
- FAQs to navigate common obstacles
- A quick reference index for ministry in the moment

You don't need to be an expert to use these tools. You just need to be willing, Spirit-led, and grounded in the Word. The Body of Christ is waiting for leaders who can say, "*Come with me. I know the way out.*"

Let's raise up a generation of freedom-bringers.

Leader's Guide Cheat Sheet

How to Walk Someone Through "Escaping the Enemy's Snares"

The following resources were created not only to help individuals find freedom but also to equip leaders, pastors, and prayer ministers to guide others through the process. Below you'll find a simple framework, red flags to listen for, and a sample walkthrough you can model

HELP SET FREE

6 Steps to Dismantling and Escaping the Snares of the Enemy

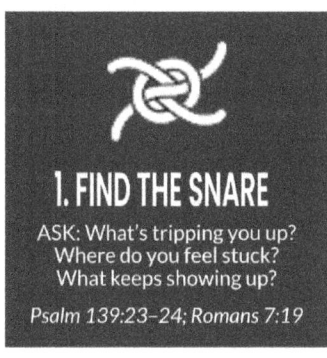

1. FIND THE SNARE

ASK: What's tripping you up? Where do you feel stuck? What keeps showing up?

Psalm 139:23-24; Romans 7:19

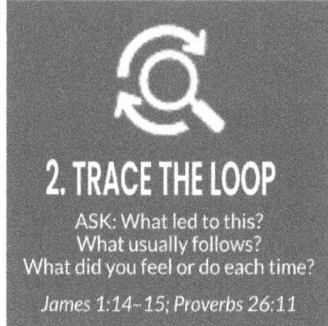

2. TRACE THE LOOP

ASK: What led to this? What usually follows? What did you feel or do each time?

James 1:14-15; Proverbs 26:11

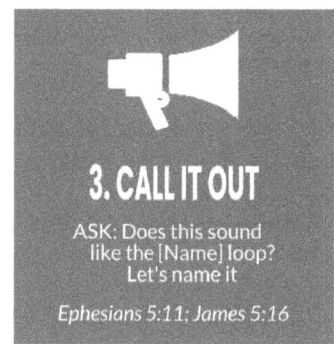

3. CALL IT OUT

ASK: Does this sound like the [Name] loop? Let's name it

Ephesians 5:11; James 5:16

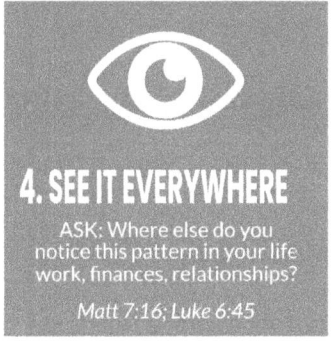

4. SEE IT EVERYWHERE

ASK: Where else do you notice this pattern in your life work, finances, relationships?

Matt 7:16; Luke 6:45

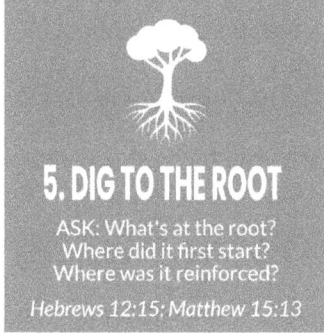

5. DIG TO THE ROOT

ASK: What's at the root? Where did it first start? Where was it reinforced?

Hebrews 12:15; Matthew 15:13

6. STEP INTO FREEDOM

- Renounce • Repent
- Forgive • Replace
- Declare • Live it

2 Corinthians 5:17; Romans 12:1-2

> ...let us throw off everything that hinders and the sin that so easily entangles. And let us run with perseverance the race marked out for us, fixing our eyes on Jesus... Hebrews 12:2

Worksheets, Declarations, Companion Sheets, and More for Download

For copies of the worksheets in this book and other resources related to your identity in Christ and learning to live in the fullness of Christ, documents associated with this book are available for download. Visit www.thedefiningplace.com/resources.

There, you can download extra worksheets, companion worksheets, and other declarations about who you are in Christ.

26 Destructive Loop Overview

1. **Abandonment Loop:** Abandonment → Fear of Being Alone → Anxiety → Clinging or Walls → Control → Disconnection → Rejection (Real or Perceived) → Offense → Unforgiveness → Hopelessness → Destruction
2. **Accusation Loop:** Pain or Insecurity → Fault-Finding → Gossip/Slander → Division → Guilt → Self-Righteousness → Blindness to Own Sin → Hardness of Heart → Defensiveness → Isolation → Rejection (real or perceived) → Accusation (of self or others) → Destruction
3. **Addiction Loop:** Pain → Escape → Temporary Relief → Guilt → Shame → Hiding → Craving → Relapse → Destruction
4. **Anger Loop:** Anger → Offense → Unforgiveness → Bitterness → Hatred → Vengeance → Murderous Thoughts → Destruction
5. **Apathy Loop:** Disappointment → Disengagement → Numbness → Lack of Motivation → Hopelessness → Inaction → Missed Purpose → Destruction
6. **Betrayal Loop:** Trust → Betrayal → Shock → Anger → Vows or Walls → Bitterness → Distrust → Isolation → Destruction
7. **Bitterness Loop:** Offense → Unforgiveness → Bitterness → Justification → Hardness of Heart → Isolation → Deception → Spiritual Blindness → Destruction
8. **Comparison Loop:** Insecurity → Comparison → Jealousy or Self-Rejection → Striving or Sabotage → Resentment → Bitterness → Shame or Pride → Destruction
9. **Control Loop:** Control → Disconnection → Rejection (Real or Perceived) → Offense → Unforgiveness → Hopelessness → Destruction
10. **Fear Loop:** Fear → Anxiety → Catastrophizing → Hesitation → Withdrawal → Missed Opportunity → Blame → Condemnation → Hopelessness → Paralysis → Destruction
11. **Grief Loop:** Grief → Numbness → Withdrawal → Suppression → Anger → Bitterness → Hopelessness → Death Agreements → Destruction
12. **Identity Confusion Loop:** Accusation / Lack of Affirmation → Confusion → People-Pleasing → Compromise → Regret → Shame → Self-Rejection → Despair → Destruction
13. **Idolatry Loop:** Discontent → Idol or Substitute Source → Temporary Relief → Attachment → Guilt → Spiritual Numbness → Hardness of Heart → Destruction
14. **Isolation Loop:** Pain or Disappointment → Withdrawal → Distrust → Self-Protection → Lack of Community → Loneliness → Despair → Destruction
15. **Numbness Loop:** Pain or Overwhelm → Emotional Numbness → Disengagement → Passivity → Isolation → Depression → Hopelessness → Destruction
16. **Overwhelm Loop:** Overwhelm → Anxiety → Control or Paralysis → Exhaustion → Despair → Hopelessness → Destruction
17. **Perfectionism or Performance:** Rejection (often through correction) → Pressure → Fear (of failure and further rejection) → Desire for Control → Lack of Trust → Overworking or Perfectionism → Exhaustion → Shame → Self-Condemnation → Burnout → Destruction
18. **Perversion Loop:** Wound or Exposure → Curiosity → Indulgence → Guilt → Shame → Secrecy → Craving → Escalation → Destruction
19. **Pride Loop:** Pride → Independence → Refusal to Receive Help → Rejection of Others → Isolation → Frustration → Stagnation → Judgment of Others → Fall/Failure → Shame → Self-Hatred → Destruction
20. **Rebellion Loop:** Wounding or Control by Others → Rebellion → Independence → Justification → Deception → Isolation → Sin Patterns → Hardness of Heart → Destruction
21. **Rejection Loop:** Rejection → Insecurity → Comparison → Self-Rejection → Isolation → Bitterness → Hatred → Destruction
22. **Self-Hatred Loop:** Abuse, Wound, or Rejection → Offense → Fear → Negative Self-Talk → Comparison → Self-Rejection → Disgust → Shame → Despair → Self-Blame → Destructive Behaviors → Reinforced Self-Hatred → Destruction
23. **Shame Loop:** Shame → Fear of Rejection → Hiding → Accusation → Self-Imposed Rejection → Control/Perfectionism → Exhaustion or Breakdown → Destruction
24. **Suppressed Anger Loop:** Anger → Silence/Suppression → Resentment → Guilt → Shame → Self-Accusation → Depression → Physical Symptoms (sickness, fatigue) → Breakdown → Destruction
25. **Trauma Loop:** Trauma → Fear → Hyper-vigilance → Isolation → Emotional Numbness → Disconnection → Despair → Destruction
26. **Victim Loop:** Injustice → Pain → Defensiveness → Offense → Justification → Blame → Powerlessness → Entitlement → Pride → Destruction

Tips for Leaders: Cultivating a Safe and Effective Environment

The process of inner healing and deliverance requires a posture of humility, safety, and Spirit-led guidance. Use these tips to ensure you are stewarding the person's journey with wisdom and grace

Be Patient — One of the greatest gifts you can give someone is unhurried presence. Don't rush to name their loop before they've had time to discover it with the Holy Spirit. Instead of offering your diagnosis, use open-ended questions: "What did you feel right before that happened?" or "What usually follows when that shame hits?" You could even ask, "Why don't you take a moment and ask the Holy Spirit to highlight what you need to focus on?"

Stay Grace-Filled & Non-Shaming — This process is about freedom, not shaming people. Never imply the person is failing or at fault for being in a loop. Acknowledge that the loops formed from a wound where they likely agreed to protect themselves. Example: "*That pattern was a learned defense mechanism that kept you safe, but now we're inviting Jesus to give you a better way.*"

Empower, Don't Rescue or Fix — Guide the individual to the Father, who is the deliverer, rescuer, and healer. Your role is that of a steward, not the solution or the hero. Remember, freedom grows with courageous honesty, practical humility, and continual practice from the person seeking help. Give them assignments and encourage them to follow through with the journal prompts and declarations between sessions.

Avoid Projecting & Stay Present — This is not about you. Don't assume your journey is the same as the person you are sitting with. Every wound and root is unique. Stay focused on their story and the patterns they reveal. If a personal memory surfaces for you, process it later—remain present with the individual.

Be Prepared to Refer Out — Bless integrated care. The tools in this book are meant to complement, not replace, professional care from licensed medical and mental-health providers. If the issues extend beyond your scope or require licensed support for conditions like severe depression, active addiction, or complex trauma, it's okay to refer them out to licensed professionals.

Be aware of Trauma-Informed Care — If strong emotions, trauma memories, or safety concerns surface, pause and follow the guidance in the *Pastoral Acknowledgment & Safety Note* (Page 4). Use the resources and warnings provided in the front of the book.

Leader's Guide

Boundaries and Safety Protocols

When ministering to others, especially in vulnerable settings, you must establish clear, godly boundaries that honor all parties.

Minister in Pairs: Whenever possible, minister in pairs. This provides spiritual covering, ensures accountability, and is practical by providing a witness.

Cross-Gender Ministry: We recommend not doing 1:1 cross-gender private sessions for several reasons. If this is unavoidable, meet in a public, visible setting.

Confidentiality: Honor confidentiality, assuring the person that their story is their story and not yours to share. Maintain confidentiality and ensure that their story is safe with you (and your ministry partner).

No Graphic Details: In small-group settings, remind participants to keep stories brief and appropriate. This is crucial for maintaining a safe relational environment and preventing unnecessary emotional exposure or trauma transfer.

Keep Jesus at the Center: Breakthrough sticks best when those in the room are safe, the steps are clear, and Jesus stays at the center. Focus on tracing the loop, repentance, forgiveness, renunciation, and the renewal of the mind. Remember, all of this is made possible only by the love of the Father, the power of the Holy Spirit, and the finished work of Christ.

Red Flags and When to Refer: (When in doubt, refer out. Integrated care addresses every area of life.)

- Active suicidal ideation or plan
- Active substance abuse requiring detox
- Severe dissociation or psychotic symptoms (hallucinations, delusions unrelated to spiritual warfare)
- Any medical/psychiatric emergency
- Severe eating disorders with medical complications
- Complex trauma requiring specialized trauma therapy

DO'S (What to Practice)

- Ask curious questions and use the "Identifying Emotions" sheet.
- Use the Quick Reference Index to look for "Red Flag Statements" that align with the person's narrative.
- Encourage the use of the companion worksheets for personal follow-through.
- Guide them to speak the declarations aloud, a key physical act of exchanging lies for truth.

DON'TS (What to Avoid)

- Don't rush forgiveness; wait for the Holy Spirit's leading and ensure the root of pain is acknowledged first.
- Don't over-interpret or force loop names. Your goal is to guide discovery, not dictate truth.
- Don't promise instant, one-session freedom. Remind them that healing often happens in the process.
- Don't counsel from your own unhealed wounds. If a person's story triggers you, seek your own support.

Leader's Guide

Time to Lead Someone To Escape and Dismantle The Enemy's Snares

1. Find the Snare (Start with the Presenting Issue)

- The presenting issue may be a recurring struggle or theme in their life. They may know what it is, or they may be unaware. You can ask the following questions to help draw the issue out.

"What brings you here?" "What are you struggling with most right now?" "Would it be ok if we take a moment and ask God if there is a pattern in our lives He wants to help us deal with?"

2. Trace the Loop (Map the Pattern)

- Guide them step by step: *"So when you feel shame, what do you usually do? And then what happens after that?"*

- Remember, a loop | cycle | pattern | stronghold is formed when:

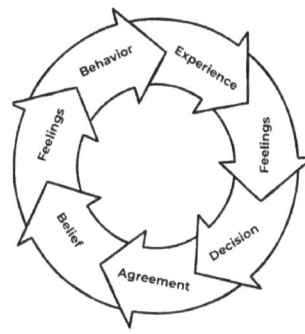

An event or experience → Causes certain feelings → Those feelings lead to a decision → That decision forms agreements in the spiritual realm → Those agreements reinforce a set of beliefs → Those beliefs lead to other feelings and behaviors → Those behaviors create experiences that reinforce the original beliefs.

"Let's take the last time you blew up. What did you feel right before you blew up at your kids? When you did blow up at them, what did you feel or think afterward? What did you do in response to that thought or feeling?

- Continue to explore before and after until the loop emerges.

3. Name the Repeating Pattern (Identify the Loop)

- Compare and match their story with the loops in this resource.
- Don't force it—sometimes two loops overlap. Choose the one that best explains the primary cycle.

"It sounds like what you've described really lines up with the Anger Loop. I'm going to read it and see if it feels accurate to you."

Leader's Guide

4. Identify Broader Presence of the Loop

- Once the loop is named, ask where else it shows up in their life. This expands awareness beyond the presenting issue and reveals how deeply it's shaping them.

- For example, Pornography may be connected to an Addiction loop, but there could also be a Perfectionism, Perversion, Rebellion, or even Isolation loop that involves the destructive behavior of pornography.

"When you look back, have you noticed this same anger pattern showing up in other relationships, jobs, or seasons?" or "Are there other times when you've withdrawn in response to hurt?"

5. Explore the Root / How It Started

- After identifying where the loop repeats, help them trace back to the original wound, lie, or agreement that opened the door.

- This is where the Holy Spirit often brings breakthrough insight.

"Why don't you ask the Lord when the first time you experienced that anger or rejection and partnered with the enemy's trap was?" or "Why don't you ask the Lord when this loop got started or how it was reinforced?"

6. Guide Them to Reset the Loop

Lead them through the Steps that Interrupt the Loop. Include:

- Renouncing lies,
- Repenting of sin,
- Forgiving,
- Inviting the Father's healing,
- Declaring truth

Encourage them to speak declarations out loud and write in the journal prompts.

7. Sample Questions and Prayers to End

- *"Is the part of you that first experienced ____ willing to risk inviting Father God to take the pain of that moment?"*

- *"Is the part of you that experienced that willing to risk inviting the Lord to come and heal it?"*

- *"Come, Heavenly Father, take the pain of what happened, heal every area of this person's life connected to or resulting from what happened, and make whole what needs to be. Help them replace all the lies, beliefs, and patterns connected to it. Forgive them for partnering with those things and rewire their brain to reflect the new reality that you are giving to them, in Jesus' name, amen."*

Quick Reference Index

General red flag statements to help leaders discern which loop may be at work.

Abandonment Loop	• "Everyone leaves me eventually." • "I can't trust people to stay." • "I'll just leave first before they hurt me."
Accusation Loop	• "They're the problem, not me." • "Everyone is against me." • "People just don't understand."
Addiction Loop	• "I'll quit tomorrow." • "I feel so guilty, but I can't stop." • "This is the only thing that helps me cope."
Anger Loop	• "They always push my buttons." • "I just explode and can't stop myself." • "People deserve what I dish out."
Apathy Loop	• "What's the point?" • "I just don't care anymore." • "Nothing ever changes."
Betrayal Loop	• "I'll never trust again." • "People always stab me in the back." • "I'll protect myself from now on."
Bitterness Loop	• "I'll never forgive them." • "They don't deserve my forgiveness." • "I'm never letting this go."
Comparison Loop	• "They're always better than me." • "I'll never measure up." • "Why can't I have what they have?"
Control Loop	• "If I don't handle it, no one else will." • "People always let me down." • "I can't relax unless I know what's happening."

Quick Reference Index

Fear Loop	• "I always think of the worst-case scenario." • "I just freeze when things get tough." • "I can't trust anyone."
Grief Loop	• "I'll never recover from this loss." • "I feel numb and empty." • "Life has no meaning anymore."
Identity Confusion Loop	• "I don't know who I really am." • "I just want people to like me." • "I feel like a different person around different people."
Idolatry Loop	• "I just need this to be happy." • "Once I get that, I'll be fulfilled." • "God isn't enough for me right now."
Isolation Loop	• "I'm better off alone." • "People just disappoint me." • "No one really understands me."
Numbness Loop	• "I feel nothing." • "It's like I'm just going through the motions." • "I don't care if I live or die."
Overwhelm Loop	• "It's too much—I can't handle this." • "I just shut down when I'm stressed." • "Everything depends on me."
Perfectionism / Performance	• "I can't stop working or everything will fall apart." • "I'm never doing enough." • "I should be beyond this by now."
Perversion Loop	• "I can't control my thoughts." • "I know it's wrong, but I keep going back." • "It's just a little fantasy—it doesn't hurt anyone."
Pride Loop	• "I don't need anyone's help." • "No one else can do it right." • "I'm fine on my own."

Quick Reference Index

Rebellion Loop	• "No one tells me what to do." • "I'll do it my way." • "Authority always abuses people."
Rejection Loop	• "I just don't feel like I belong anywhere." • "No matter what, people always end up leaving me." • "I'm probably not good enough for them anyway."
Self-Hatred Loop	• "I'm disgusting." • "Everything is my fault." • "I hate myself."
Shame Loop	• "If people really knew me, they'd leave." • "I'm not enough." • "I have to be perfect or I'll be rejected."
Suppressed Anger Loop	• "I'm fine." (when clearly not fine) • "I just keep it inside." • "I don't want to rock the boat."
Trauma Loop	• "I just want to feel safe again." • "I always feel on edge." • "I can't stop reliving what happened."
Victim Loop	• "They did this to me." • "I'll never get ahead because of them." • "It's all their fault."

A Case Study: Dismantling the Snares of Addiction, Perversion, and Perfectionism

As a pastor and former program manager for addiction recovery, I've seen firsthand how the enemy uses specific traps to keep people in bondage. We know about the destructive loops—those subtle yet powerful patterns that hold us captive. But knowing about them is only the first step; the real work is learning to recognize them and helping others overcome them.

Let's walk through a real-life example, a composite of conversations I've had many times. The name and details have been changed, but the pattern is all too common.

Feeling the Snare and Tracing the Loop

I'm sitting down with a man named Mark, who feels like he's constantly hitting a wall. He comes to me feeling defeated and stuck.

- **Me**: "Mark, what's been on your heart?"

- **Mark**: "I keep screwing up. I get free for a while, but then I go right back to looking at porn. I feel like a complete failure."

- **Me**: "Thank you for that courage. Let's trace this back. Just before you looked at it, what were you feeling?"

- **Mark**: "I was feeling stressed and overwhelmed. My wife had been going off on me again, and I just felt like I could never measure up."

- **Me**: "So you felt rejected. Where did that feeling lead you?"

- **Mark**: "I just wanted to get away. I went to the other room to be by myself. I wasn't even planning to look at porn; I just started scrolling on my phone, and it was a way to numb the pain. For a moment, it felt good because I wasn't thinking about how bad I felt."

- **Me**: "I hear you. So you're feeling rejected, you retreat, and you find a temporary escape. Then what happens after you look at it?"

- **Mark**: "I feel disgusting. The relief is gone, and I'm hit with a wave of guilt and shame. I take a shower, hide my phone, and promise myself I'll never do it again. But the shame just makes me pull away from my wife even more, and the cycle starts all over."

Calling It Out and Seeing It Everywhere

By tracing the pattern, we've identified three powerful loops at work, all interconnected.

- **Me**: "Mark, I hear you. The enemy has set some specific traps for you, and we're going to call them out by name. I see three distinct patterns here.
    - **The Addiction Loop:** You feel pain from rejection, so you escape to temporary relief (scrolling and porn), which leads to guilt, shame, and hiding, ultimately fueling a craving that brings you right back to relapse.
    - **The Perversion Loop:** You experience a wound, and rather than dealing with it, you let curiosity lead you to indulge in something you know is wrong. This creates guilt and shame, which you hide, causing the craving to escalate and the cycle to repeat.
    - **The Perfectionism Loop:** Feeling rejected creates pressure to be perfect for your wife. You strive to measure up, but when you fall short, you feel exhausted and overwhelmed. This leads to shame and self-condemnation, which pushes you further into the escape."
- **Mark**: "Wow. I've never seen it like that. It's not just about the porn; it's about not being enough."
- **Me**: "That's right. The addiction isn't the root; it's a symptom. The real starting point here is the pain of rejection. It's what sends you spiraling down these destructive highways. Where else have you noticed this pattern in your life? This fear of rejection or feeling like you can't measure up?"
- **Mark**: "At work, I'm under so much stress to perform and not fail that when I get home, I just want to shut down. I've never connected that my fear of rejection at work might be fueling my struggle at home."

DIGGING TO THE ROOT

Once the loops are named, it's time to go deeper and find the root. This is where we invite the Holy Spirit to reveal the starting point.

- **Me**: "Let's ask the Lord to take us back to the very first time you felt this kind of rejection, before it became a pattern."

I pause and wait for the Spirit to speak. After a moment, Mark's eyes open.

- **Mark**: "He just brought to mind when I was in first grade. I tried out for the basketball team. All my friends made it, but I was cut. They made fun of me, and I felt so rejected. I pretended I was fine, but I wasn't."

- **Me**: "I hear you. That moment planted a seed of a lie in your heart: 'You'll never be enough.' And the enemy has been reinforcing that lie in every area of your life ever since. Do you see the connection?"

- **Mark**: "Yes, I do."

STEPPING INTO FREEDOM

We've exposed the root and named the snare. Now, we are ready to take action and walk into freedom.

- **Me**: "Mark, we're not just going to talk about this; we're going to dismantle it strategically. Are you willing to forgive those friends for the way they made you feel? And are you willing to let go of the pain and offense?"

- **Mark**: "Yes."

- **Me**: "Next, are you willing to renounce the lie that your identity and worth are defined by what you do or what other people think about you?"

- **Mark**: "Yes."

- **Me**: "Finally, are you willing to ask God to heal the wound that first took root in your heart? And are you willing to learn new ways of responding when you feel hurt or rejected?"

- **Mark**: "Yes, I am."

We then pray together, inviting the Father to come and take away the pain, heal the wound, and replace the old lies with His truth. I remind him that he is a son of the King, deeply loved and fully accepted.

- **Me**: "We just identified and began to break a spiritual stronghold. This is where we start building. We'll set up some simple, clear next steps for you to take, anchored in the truth of God's Word. Remember, freedom isn't an event; it's a journey, and you are no longer alone on this path."

A Second Case Study: Dismantling the Snares of Perfectionism, Shame, and Suppressed Anger

This case study is a composite based on common patterns to illustrate how multiple destructive loops can intertwine, focusing on the dynamic of internal pressure and emotional suppression.

FEELING THE SNARE AND TRACING THE LOOP

I'm sitting down with Sarah, a volunteer ministry leader who has recently experienced a major emotional breakdown, feeling paralyzed and unable to continue her work.

- **Me**: "Sarah, what's been on your heart? What led up to this exhaustion and inability to lead?"

- **Sarah**: "I crashed. I had a huge project deadline, and I was up all night trying to fix every tiny detail. I did it, but the next morning, I couldn't get out of bed. I was supposed to lead worship that night, but I felt so angry at the thought of having to put on a happy face and perform."

- **Me**: "That's a lot of pressure. Let's trace back from the anger. What did you do with that anger when it first hit?"

- **Sarah**: "I immediately swallowed it. I told myself, 'You're being ungrateful; a good leader wouldn't be this frustrated.' Then came the shame because I missed the worship practice—I felt like a hypocrite and a total failure."

- **Me**: "So you felt angry at the pressure, suppressed it, and it turned into shame. What did you start telling yourself after the shame hit?"

- **Sarah**: "That I can't let anyone see this weakness, or they'll realize I'm not fit to lead. I have to be the perfect, joyful one. I started meticulously planning the next project to prove to everyone—and myself—that I'm okay."

- **Me**: "I hear you. So you're feeling pressure, suppressing anger, and covering shame with performance, which drives you to exhaustion, leaving you angry and ready to crash again. What happened the first time you felt like your own emotional needs were 'too much'?"

CALLING IT OUT AND SEEING IT EVERYWHERE

By tracing the pattern, we've identified three powerful loops at work, all interconnected.

- **Me**: "Sarah, we need to call out the traps the enemy has set for you by name. We've seen three patterns in what you described:
    - **The Perfectionism/Performance Loop:** The correction (or even just the pressure to perform) creates fear of failure and a desire for control, leading to overworking and ultimately exhaustion and burnout.
    - **The Shame Loop:** A mistake or perceived failure triggers shame and fear of rejection, leading you to hide and use perfectionism (control) to cope.
    - **The Suppressed Anger Loop:** The intense pressure and lack of rest create anger, but you immediately choose silence/suppression, which ferments into resentment and then guilt and shame toward yourself.
- **Sarah**: "Wow! I didn't realize until now how much of my stress and need for control was driven by being angry that I couldn't be enough for everyone."
- **Me**: "It appears that way. The relentless drive to succeed and resentment seem to stem from a fear of not being loved and the fear of rejection if you're not perfect. Does that all track?
- **Sarah**: "YES! So many of the things I've been battling make sense now."
- **Me**: Where else does this pattern show up? Maybe it doesn't end the same way, but it's that same internal tension?"
- **Sarah**: "In my marriage. I get furious when my husband doesn't notice how hard I'm working, but I never say anything. I just reorganized a closet instead. It's my way of silently saying, 'I'm handling everything,' and 'You don't even try.'"

DIGGING TO THE ROOT

Once the loops are named, it's time to find the root. Take a moment and invite the Holy Spirit to reveal the starting point..

- **Me**: "Let's ask the Lord to take us back to the first time you felt this intense pressure to perform or felt like your anger wasn't allowed."

- **Sarah (after a moment)**: "What comes to mind is when I was in middle school. I brought home a B on a test, and my dad looked so disappointed. He said, 'I know you can do better.' In that moment, I promised myself I'd never disappoint him or myself again. I don't think I realized it, but I believed the lie that my performance determines my value, and disappointment equals rejection."
- **Me**: "That sounds like it.. So, a wound of rejection, perceived through disappointment, planted a root lie that you must perform for acceptance."
- **Sarah**: "Yeah. Wow, saying that sounds so funny, but that's exactly what happened. And it's wild because that lie is what made me start to believe 'I must be perfect to be loved or approved.'"
- **Me**: "And it sounds like you've been working yourself to exhaustion to prove that ever since."
- **Sarah**: "Wow! All to keep that stupid promise."

STEPPING INTO FREEDOM

We've exposed the root and named the snare. Now, we take action to walk into freedom.

- **Me**: "Sarah, you've done a lot of work, but now we're going to continue to dismantle this stronghold. Are you willing to forgive your father for tying your worth to your performance and for making you feel unsafe in your imperfection?"
- **Sarah**: "Yes, I am. Heavenly Father, I choose to forgive my father for the way he looked at me and for tying my worth to my performance. I forgive him for making me feel unsafe. I choose to hand him along with all the emotions, looks, wounds, fears, and sense of rejection that are connected to him, over to you now, Lord. Forgive me for holding resentment in my heart. In Jesus' name, Amen."
- **Me**: "Excellent! Now, let's renounce the lie that your identity is tied to your work or the approval of others.
- **Sarah**: "Absolutely! I renounce the lie that my identity or worth is tied to my work or the approval of others. And while it is ok for me to want others to accept me, my worth is already fixed in Christ."
- **Me**: "That's amazing, Sarah. Great job. Let's take it one step further. Are you willing to ask God to heal the wound from that moment when you were a middle schooler and learn new, life-giving ways of handling anger, pressure, and rest?"

- **Sarah**: "Absolutely. I'm tired of working so hard to feel loved."

We then pray together, inviting the Father to take away the pain, heal the wound, and replace the old lies with His truth: "I am accepted and approved in Christ, not by performance".

- **Me**: "Sarah, I'm really proud of you. You've shown a lot of courage today. I want you to remember, though, freedom is a journey, not an event."
- **Sarah**: "I'm realizing that now."
- **Me**: "This week, your new step of obedience is this: When you feel the pressure to perform rise, stop what you're doing, acknowledge the anger honestly, and ask God for permission to rest before you take another step. Will you commit to that?"
- **Sarah**: "Yes. Thank you for walking me through this."

This deliberate shift forces Sarah to interrupt the loop (stopping the performance) and replace the old lie (I must earn love) with a new, Spirit-led response (I can rest because I am already loved).

Living in and From Freedom

What Comes Next?

Breaking free from destructive loops is just the beginning. Here's how to maintain freedom:

1. **Daily Declarations** - Make them part of your morning routine
2. **Consistent Check-Ins** - Use the tracking worksheets weekly or monthly with a small group
3. **Community** - Stay connected; isolation reopens loops
4. **When Loops Resurface** - Use the 5-Minute RESET immediately
5. **Ongoing Discipleship** - Freedom grows in relationship with Jesus and His people

Next Steps:

- **Continue tracking progress monthly.** Remember, freedom is proven over time.
- **Share your breakthrough with a safe community.** Testimonies have a way of establishing the breakthrough in our lives and in the lives of those who hear them.
- **Consider how God might use your freedom to help others.** Your freedom isn't just yours; it is meant for the body of Christ and those who will one day be a part of the body. Consider helping others walk through this.
- **Explore our other resources.** We have a growing library of resources.

Remember: You're not just getting free—you're learning to LIVE free and carry His kingdom.

Frequently Asked Questions

About This Resource

Is this book only for people with "serious" problems? No. These loops affect everyone at different levels. You might recognize subtle patterns of control, comparison, or perfectionism that you've never named before. This book is for anyone who wants to live in greater freedom—whether you're dealing with mild frustration or deep bondage.

Do I need to work through all 26 loops? No. Start with the one that feels most active in your life right now. Many people find that 2-4 loops are interconnected. Focus on those, and you'll often see a breakthrough in multiple areas.

Can I use this book on my own, or do I need a leader/pastor? Both work. The book is designed for personal use and includes worksheets and the RESET framework. However, walking through it with a trusted friend, small group, or ministry leader can provide accountability, prayer support, and deeper insight.

How long does it take to break free from a loop? Freedom is a journey, not a single event. Some people experience immediate breakthrough; others find freedom unfolds in layers over weeks or months. The key is consistent practice: daily declarations, weekly check-ins, and ongoing dependence on the Holy Spirit.

What if I don't "feel" anything when I pray through the steps? Emotional highs don't always accompany freedom. Sometimes it's a quiet, steady shift. Trust the process, keep declaring truth, and watch for fruit over time, such as changes in how you respond to triggers, increased peace, and healthier relationships.

About Deliverance & Spiritual Warfare

Is this book about "casting out demons"? Partly. This book addresses both deliverance (removing demonic influence) and dismantling strongholds (thought patterns and beliefs that remain after deliverance). Many people need both. Casting out a demon without renewing the mind leaves the door open for it to return (Matthew 12:43-45).

If you have questions about deliverance, we recommend **Deliverance Demystified: Unlocking Biblical Answers to Real Questions for Lasting Freedom.**

If you want the tools to help you lead deliverances more effectively, grab ***The Deliverance and Inner Healing Manual: A Spirit-Empowered Guide to Unlocking Biblical Freedom and Wholeness***.

I've been through deliverance before, but I'm still struggling. Why? Deliverance removes demonic influence, but it doesn't automatically dismantle the strongholds (beliefs, agreements, and patterns) that were built in partnership with that influence. This book helps you identify and tear down those structures and replace them with truth.

Can a Christian have a demon? Christians cannot be possessed (owned) by demons, but they can be oppressed or influenced by them—especially in areas where doors have been opened through sin, trauma, or agreements with lies. The Holy Spirit seals your spirit, but your soul (mind, will, emotions) can still be a battleground.

What if I'm skeptical about deliverance ministry? That's okay. This book emphasizes Scripture, the Holy Spirit's leading, and practical steps anyone can take. You don't have to embrace every deliverance practice to benefit from identifying destructive patterns, renouncing lies, and renewing your mind. Try the RESET framework and see what God does.

Is this book charismatic/Pentecostal? The content is rooted in Scripture and accessible across denominational lines. While the author is Spirit-filled and embraces the gifts of the Holy Spirit, the tools—repentance, forgiveness, renouncing lies, declaring truth—are biblical practices for all believers.

About Therapy & Professional Care

Does this book replace therapy or medication? Absolutely not. This resource complements professional care—it doesn't replace it. If you're dealing with clinical depression, trauma, suicidal thoughts, or other mental health concerns, please work with licensed professionals alongside using these tools.

Should I stop taking my medication if I go through deliverance? No. Never stop or change medication without consulting your prescribing clinician. God works through medicine, therapy, and spiritual ministry. We bless integrated care.

When should I seek professional help instead of (or in addition to) using this book? Seek professional help if you're experiencing:

- Persistent depression, anxiety, or panic attacks
- Thoughts of self-harm or suicide
- Trauma flashbacks or PTSD symptoms
- Substance misuse or eating disorders
- Any symptom that concerns you or those who love you

If you're in crisis (U.S.): Call or text 988 | If in immediate danger: 911

Practical Application

What's the difference between the 6-Step Process and the 5-Minute RESET? The **6-Step Process** (Find, Trace, Call Out, See Everywhere, Dig to Root, Step Into Freedom) is comprehensive—ideal for deep work in a ministry session or personal study. The **5-Minute RESET** (Recognize, Expose, Submit, Exchange, Take a step) is for immediate intervention when you feel triggered, tempted, or stuck.

How do I know which loop I'm in? Start by identifying the "fruit"—the behavior or struggle that keeps showing up (anger outbursts, perfectionism, withdrawal, porn use, etc.). Then use the "[Trace the Loop" worksheet](#)" to map what typically triggers it and what follows. Match your pattern to the loop descriptions in [Part 2](#).

What if I identify with multiple loops? That's common. Loops often overlap and feed into each other (e.g., Rejection → Perfectionism → Shame → Isolation). Start with the loop that feels most frequent or intense. As you address the root of one, others often loosen.

Do I have to forgive people who deeply hurt me? Yes—but forgiveness is for *your* freedom, not their approval. Forgiveness doesn't mean reconciliation, trust, or saying "it was okay." It means releasing them from the debt they owe you and entrusting justice to God (Romans 12:19). Unforgiveness keeps *you* in prison.

What if I can't remember a specific "root" event? That's okay. Sometimes the Holy Spirit reveals a specific memory; other times, He highlights a pattern or theme (e.g., "You've always felt like you had to earn love"). Trust His leading. You don't need perfect recall to experience freedom—just honest acknowledgment of the lie and a willingness to exchange it for truth.

What do I do after I've worked through a loop? A:

1. **Daily**: Use the [morning check-in (page 67)](#) and [evening check-in (page 68)](#) worksheets and speak the declarations aloud
2. **Weekly**: Review your [30-Day Tracker (page 69)](#) and celebrate progress
3. **Monthly**: Revisit the loop chapter and journal on areas of growth
4. **Ongoing**: Stay connected to community, keep renewing your mind, and watch for old patterns trying to resurface

For Leaders & Ministry Use

Can I use this material in my church or ministry? Yes, with proper credit. This book is copyrighted, so you cannot reproduce entire sections without permission. However, you may:

- Teach from it in small groups or classes
- Use the framework and concepts in ministry settings
- Reference and recommend it to others
- Download worksheets from www.thedefiningplace.com/resources for ministry use

Do I need special training to help someone through this? You don't need formal credentials, but you should:

- Be walking in your own freedom and emotional health
- Have a pastoral heart and be Spirit-led
- Understand boundaries (ministry in pairs, avoid cross-gender 1:1 private sessions)
- Know when to refer someone to professional care
- Read the Leader's Guide (Part 4) carefully

What if someone has a strong emotional reaction or manifestation during ministry? Stay calm, pastoral, and Spirit-led. Keep the person focused on Jesus, not the manifestation. Speak truth, make short and authoritative commands and prayers, and avoid theatrics. If someone becomes unsafe or you're out of your depth, pause and refer to a more experienced leader or professional.

How do I know if someone needs deliverance, inner healing, or both? Most people need both. If there's demonic influence, address it through deliverance. If there's a wound, lie, or unprocessed emotion, address it through inner healing. Often, you'll move back and forth between the two in the same session. Follow the Holy Spirit's lead.

About Declarations & Renewing the Mind

Why do I need to speak declarations out loud? Speaking truth aloud engages your mind, emotions, and physical body in agreement with God's Word. It's a warfare tactic (Revelation 12:11), a faith exercise (Romans 10:17), and a way to interrupt old thought patterns. Your enemy listens, and so does your own soul.

How long should I keep declaring truth over myself? Until the truth becomes more real to you than the lie. This could be days, weeks, or months. Think of it like physical therapy—you don't stop just because you feel better once. Keep building strength until the new pattern is established.

What if I don't believe the declarations yet? Speak them anyway. Faith isn't about feeling; it's about aligning with truth. As you consistently declare God's Word, your beliefs will catch up. This is the process of renewing the mind (Romans 12:2).

Troubleshooting

What if I relapse or fall back into an old pattern after I thought I was free? Relapse doesn't mean failure—freedom is a journey, and setbacks often reveal deeper layers that need healing. Here's what to do:

1. **Don't hide in shame.** Bring it into the light immediately with God and a trusted person (Romans 8:1).
2. **Ask what the relapse reveals.** What triggered it? What were you feeling? What lie did you believe in that moment?
3. **Run the RESET immediately. Recognize** the loop, **Expose** the lie, **Submit** it to Jesus, **Exchange** it for truth, and **Take** one interrupt step.
4. **Revisit the root.** Go back to Step 5 Dig to the Root (page 63-64). There may be a deeper layer or a different entry point to address.
5. **Strengthen your disciplines.** Are you speaking declarations daily (page 66)? Staying in community? Avoiding triggers? Freedom requires ongoing practice.
6. **Get back up quickly.** Proverbs 24:16 says the righteous fall seven times but rise again. The key is not perfection—it's getting back up fast and running to Jesus.
7. **Consider additional support.** If relapse becomes a pattern, work with a ministry leader, counselor, or recovery program. There's no shame in needing more help.

Remember: Every time you repent and return to Jesus, you're building resilience and deepening dependence on Him. The goal isn't sinless perfection. Instead, it's a life marked by humility, trust, and forward movement.

"The Lord upholds all who fall and lifts up all who are bowed down." — Psalm 145:14

I've worked through the steps, but I still feel stuck. What now? Consider these possibilities:

- There may be another loop underneath (keep digging)
- You may need to work with a ministry leader or counselor
- You may need professional help for trauma or mental health concerns
- You may need deliverance from a specific demonic influence
- You may need to slow down and let the Holy Spirit work more deeply in one area before moving on

What if painful memories surface that I wasn't expecting? This is normal in the healing process. Pause, invite the Holy Spirit into that memory, and ask Jesus to show you where He was in that moment. If it feels overwhelming, reach out to a trusted friend, leader, or counselor. Don't try to process deep trauma alone.

Can I be free if I've been in this pattern for decades? Yes. No pattern is too old, too deep, or too intense for Jesus to break. Some of the most powerful testimonies come from people who've been bound for years. The key is staying consistent, staying connected to community, and trusting the process.

Final Encouragement

Remember:

- Freedom is a journey, not an event
- Jesus has already won the victory (Colossians 2:15)
- The Holy Spirit is your helper, counselor, and guide (John 14:26)
- You were made for freedom—don't settle for less (Galatians 5:1)
- Small, consistent steps lead to lasting transformation

"So if the Son sets you free, you will be free indeed." — John 8:36

For more resources, visit www.thedefiningplace.com

Glossary

Abandonment Loop	A destructive pattern triggered by a real or perceived emotional or physical loss that leads to a fear of being alone, resulting in clinging, walls, and control.
Accusation Loop	A destructive pattern driven by pain or insecurity that expresses itself through fault-finding, gossip, or slander, leading to defensiveness, isolation, and self-righteousness.
Addiction Loop	A destructive pattern triggered by pain, stress, or emptiness that seeks temporary relief through escape behaviors, leading to shame, hiding, and relapse.
Agreement	An internal or spiritual choice to believe a lie, accept a false identity, or enter into a destructive pattern. Agreements often reinforce negative beliefs and power destructive loops.
Alter/Part	A fragmented part of a person formed through trauma, fear, grief, drug use, or unprocessed emotion typically to protect the person emotionally or psychologically. In healing, Jesus brings these parts back into alignment with the person's God-given identity.
Anger Loop	A destructive pattern triggered by offense that spirals through unforgiveness, bitterness, hatred, and vengeance.
Apathy Loop	A destructive pattern characterized by disappointment leading to disengagement, numbness, and ultimately inaction and missed purpose.
Authority (Spiritual)	The power and right believers are given through Jesus Christ's finished work to recognize, resist, break free from, and dismantle every plan of the enemy.
Betrayal Loop	A destructive pattern initiated by broken trust leads to shock, anger, inner vows/walls, distrust, and eventual isolation.

Glossary

Bitterness Loop	A destructive pattern caused by unforgiveness that hardens the heart through justification and isolation, resulting in spiritual blindness.
Catastrophizing	A mental stage within the Fear Loop where anxiety triggers the mind to jump to and focus on the worst-case scenario quickly.
Comparison Loop	A destructive pattern driven by insecurity that leads to jealousy/self-rejection, causing striving, resentment, or sabotage.
Control Loop	A destructive pattern where anxiety and uncertainty drive the person to micromanage people or circumstances, leading to disconnection and rejection.
Curses	A curse is a spiritually charged word, agreement, or consequence that invites demonic oppression or influence on people, places, and objects. Curses can come through patterns of habitual sin, authority figures, spoken words, rituals, or self-agreement and must be broken by the blood and authority of Jesus.
Deliverance	Partnering with Jesus to identify and remove anything that has slowed us down or entangled us. It involves breaking agreements with lies and sin, closing open doors, casting out the demonic, learning to live in God's truth, and partnering with the establishment of God's love and Kingdom.
Destructive Loop	A subtle, repeating pattern of thought, feeling, and behavior, often involving a wound, a lie, and a decision, that steals freedom, distorts identity, and hinders relationships with God and others.
Discipleship	We define a disciple as one who is following Jesus, being changed by Jesus, and then partnering with the Father on Mission. Discipleship, therefore, is the act of being a disciple while also intentionally walking with and leading others on that journey.

Glossary

Fear Loop	A destructive pattern triggered by an unexpected threat (real or perceived) that causes anxiety and catastrophizing, often leading to hesitation, withdrawal, and paralysis.
Grief Loop	A destructive pattern initiated by loss that results in numbness and withdrawal, leading to suppression, anger, and hopelessness.
Ground	Ground is the unresolved emotional, spiritual, or relational territory where demonic influence hides or anchors itself. These are places where the enemy has been invited, allowed, or tolerated. Deliverance addresses the root, not just the fruit.
Hiding	The internal or external behavior of concealing a struggle, shame, or wound, which often leads to isolation and fuels the craving for escape in addictive or perversion loops.
Identity Confusion Loop	A destructive pattern triggered by criticism/lack of affirmation causes people-pleasing and compromise, leading to shame and self-rejection.
Idolatry Loop	A destructive pattern driven by discontent where a person turns to a substitute source (e.g., person, achievement) instead of God for temporary relief, resulting in spiritual numbness.
Inner Healing	The ministry of inviting God's presence and truth to touch and restore the deepest places of our souls to heal emotional and spiritual wounds (often trauma or relational pain).
Interrupt Step (Life-Giving Step)	A specific, simple act of active obedience chosen in partnership with the Holy Spirit (the "T" in RESET is 'Take a Next Step') to intentionally break a destructive pattern and establish a new, Spirit-led response that leads to life rather than death.
Isolation Loop	A destructive pattern triggered by pain or disappointment that leads to withdrawal, distrust, and ultimately a complete lack of community.

Glossary

Key Demon	The "key" demon is the central influence—when it's addressed, everything else starts to unravel. It's often the strongman or a major root issue that links and empowers others.
Legal Right	A legal right is any unresolved sin, vow, curse, or agreement that gives the enemy permission to remain. The enemy is a legalist. He stays where we've left doors open or made agreements with lies. But those rights are canceled at the cross when exposed and renounced.
Lie (The Enemy's)	A false statement or belief—often sown into a person's heart after a wound—that sets itself up against the knowledge of God and becomes the root of destructive behavior.
Loop	A loop is a demonic cycle that keeps people stuck in emotional or spiritual patterns like fear, shame, or rejection. Each loop has a beginning, a progression, and an end—usually destruction. Naming the loop helps us stop the cycle and reset in truth.
Manifestation	Manifestations are bodily, emotional, or verbal reactions that may surface during deliverance. They are not the goal or evidence of a successful deliverance. Instead of focusing on whether manifestations are present, fix your eyes on Jesus and partner with the Father through the power of the Holy Spirit.
Numbness Loop	A destructive pattern where pain or overwhelm is managed by emotional shutdown, leading to disengagement, passivity, and ultimately depression.
Open Door	An open door is any access point the enemy has used to enter or return, often through sin, wounds, generational iniquity, or occult involvement. A healthy deliverance should involve identifying and closing those doors with repentance, truth, and authority, and then casting out the demons that gained access through those open doors.

Glossary

Overwhelm Loop	A destructive pattern caused by excessive pressures that triggers anxiety and leads to coping mechanisms like control or paralysis, resulting in exhaustion and despair.
Perfectionism or Performance Loop	A destructive pattern rooted in rejection or fear of failure that drives a person to overwork, control, and strive to prove worth, leading to exhaustion and shame.
Perversion Loop	A destructive pattern initiated by a wound or exposure that leads through curiosity and indulgence, fueled by guilt, shame, and secrecy.
Post-Deliverance Stronghold	A deep-seated pattern of thought, belief, or response (we call them loops) that remains intact after demonic influence has been removed, leaving a place the enemy prefers to return to.
Pride Loop	A destructive pattern characterized by self-reliance and a refusal to receive help, leading to isolation, judgment of others, and ultimate failure.
Rebellion Loop	A destructive pattern triggered by wounding or control by others that results in independence, justification, and a hardness of heart toward authority.
Rejection Loop	A destructive pattern initiated by feeling unwanted or overlooked that breeds insecurity, self-rejection, and spirals into isolation and bitterness.
Renewal of the Mind	The New Testament process of being transformed by intentionally replacing old lies, agreements, and thought patterns with God's truth and declarations.
Renunciation	A spiritual act of breaking agreement with lies, inner vows, or demonic influence. This is the step of declaring, "I no longer agree with this lie".
Repentance	A spiritual act of changing one's mind and turning from sin to return to God. In the context of loops, it means confessing the ways one has partnered with the destructive pattern.

Glossary

RESET	The 5-Minute Quickstart process (Recognize, Expose, Submit, Exchange, Take a next step) is designed for quick intervention when you feel stuck, overwhelmed, or tempted.
Root (of the Snare)	The original wound, lie, or spiritual agreement—often planted in childhood or a moment of significance from which the visible, destructive snare (or fruit) of sin and behavior develops.
Self-Hatred Loop	A destructive pattern where an initial wound/rejection leads to negative self-talk and self-blame, deepening shame, and destructive behaviors.
Self-Protection	The defensive act of creating emotional walls, withdrawing, or striving for control to prevent future hurt often becomes the fuel for the Isolation, Abandonment, or Control Loops.
Shame	In the context of loops or destructive patterns, shame is a painful emotion that says, "I am a mistake," whereas guilt says, "I made a mistake." Shame leads to hiding, self-rejection, and fuels the need for control or perfectionism. In the context of deliverance, shame can be an emotion, a spirit, or a stronghold.
Snares (Enemy's)	The overarching term for the traps, entanglements, and subtle patterns the enemy uses to steal freedom and keep believers bound.
Stronghold	Strongholds are patterns of thought, belief, or action that have been built over time, often in partnership with the demonic. They usually feel protective or natural, but they actually keep people in bondage. They're torn down by truth, repentance, and God's love.

Glossary

Strongman	A strongman is the primary ruling spirit behind a demonic structure or system. It's the demon that everything else can be bound to. The strongman demon is often connected to generational patterns, major trauma, or identity lies. Jesus referred to the strongman in Matthew 12:29—"first bind the strongman, then plunder his house." In deliverance, identifying and binding the strongman leads to breakthroughs across multiple areas.
Suppressed Anger Loop	A destructive pattern where anger is met with silence/suppression, leading to hidden resentment, guilt, and shame, which often manifests as depression or physical sickness.
Trace the Loop	The process of mapping the sequence of experience, feelings, decisions, agreements, and behaviors that repeat in a destructive cycle.
Trace the Loop	The deliberate process of mapping the sequence of experience → feelings → decision → agreement that repeats in a destructive pattern to find the root.
Trauma Loop	A destructive pattern triggered by a painful, sudden, or deeply wounding event that forces the person into a survival mode of fear, hyper-vigilance, and emotional numbness.
Victim Loop	A destructive pattern triggered by injustice or pain that leads to defensiveness, justification, blame, and an overall sense of powerlessness or entitlement.
Wound	A deeply painful emotional or spiritual injury (e.g., betrayal, rejection, trauma, abuse) that, if left unhealed, becomes the starting point for a destructive loop.

Other Resources

Resource	Purpose	Who It's For
Deliverance Demystified: Unlocking Biblical Answers to Real Questions for Lasting Freedom	Understand deliverance (FAQ)	Curious, skeptical, seeking understanding
The Deliverance and Inner Healing Manual: A *Spirit-Empowered Guide to Unlocking Biblical Freedom and Wholeness.*	How to do deliverance	Practitioners, ministers, small group leaders, etc.
Undoing Enemy's Snares	POST-deliverance work to tear down strongholds	Everyone - individuals after a deliverance session + leaders taking others through deliverance
Undoing Enemy's Snares Workbook Edition	POST-deliverance work to tear down strongholds. Multiple copies of worksheets included	Everyone - individuals after a deliverance session + leaders taking others through deliverance
Declarations of Overcomers: Daily Truths to Anchor Your Identity in Christ (Print and Audio Versions)	POST-Deliverance work to renew your mind.	Everyone - individuals after a deliverance session + leaders taking others through deliverance

Online Coaching, Live Training Events, Cohorts, etc.

Coming soon:
- A book on hearing the voice of God
- A course on intercession
- Material on Healings and Miracles

Deliverance Demystified: Unlocking Biblical Answers to Real Questions for Lasting Freedom

Deliverance Demystified cuts through confusion and fear to bring biblical clarity to one of the most misunderstood areas of the Christian life. With compassion and truth, this accessible guide answers over 100 real questions about demons, strongholds, spiritual warfare, and inner healing. Whether you're curious, cautious, or called to this ministry, you'll find grounded insights, honest testimonies, and practical steps for lasting freedom in Christ. Perfect for individuals, small groups, or churches beginning the journey into Spirit-empowered deliverance.

The Deliverance and Inner Healing Manual: A Spirit-Empowered Guide to Unlocking Biblical Freedom and Wholeness.

This hands-on manual equips believers and leaders with the tools, language, and strategies needed to partner with the Holy Spirit in deliverance and inner healing ministry. Packed with step-by-step models, prayer prompts, theological foundations, diagrams, and real-life ministry stories, this guide is a trusted companion for those helping others find freedom and restoration. Whether you're leading a session, training a team, or seeking a breakthrough in your own life, this manual will help you minister with clarity, confidence, and compassion.

Declarations of Overcomers: Daily Truths to Anchor Your Identity in Christ (Print)

A powerful tool designed to help you break free from lies and anchor your heart in God's Word. Born out of real-life deliverance and inner healing, these daily declarations give you language to align your thoughts and words with the truth of Scripture and renew your mind in Christ. Each statement is rooted in God's Word, crafted to restore your identity, renew your thinking, and help you live from a place of victory.

Declarations of Overcomers: Spoken Truths to Anchor Your Identity in Christ (Audio)

A spoken word audio of our declarations. Whether you play it on repeat during prayer, in the car, or as part of your daily routine, these spoken truths will help renew your mind, strengthen your spirit, and anchor your life in Christ's victory. Each track leads you to hear God's Word declared over your life, restoring your identity and silencing the lies of the enemy.

About the Author

Jared Gregory is a pastor, author, and ministry leader who has been serving in pastoral and leadership roles since 2005. In 2009, he became a licensed minister with the Missionary Church and has since served as a lead pastor, church planter, and overseen multi-campus ministry settings. For several years, Jared helped lead an addiction recovery program, where he first encountered the transformative power of deliverance ministry. What began as a personal breakthrough became a deeper call to help others find freedom from spiritual oppression, emotional wounds, and generational strongholds.

Today, Jared co-leads The Defining Place with his wife, Leah. It is a Spirit-led ministry devoted to deliverance, healing, and equipping the Body of Christ to walk in actual spiritual authority. Jared's heart burns to see God's people walk in the fullness of His love, power, and presence. His calling is marked by five key expressions: empowering, restoring, reforming, living in the fullness of God, and catalyzing transformation.

He equips individuals and churches with practical tools and biblical truth, restores hope to broken hearts and systems, and challenges the Church to reimagine what freedom and discipleship honestly look like. Jared is a catalyst at heart—unafraid to confront the darkness, pioneer new territory, and call forth the beauty of Christ's Bride.

Jared and Leah are passionate about raising a Kingdom-centered family, rooted in the love of God, healing, and truth.

www.ingramcontent.com/pod-product-compliance
Lightning Source LLC
Chambersburg PA
CBHW050455110426

42743CB00017B/3369